It Takes More Than Concrete

How to Build a Construction Business From the Ground Up

It Takes More Than Concrete

How to Build a Construction Business
From the Ground Up

DR. ROBERT L. BOWEN, P.E.

BOOK PUBLISHING

Published & distributed by:
Dr. Robert L. Bowen, P.E.

in association with:
IBJ Book Publishing
41 E. Washington St., Suite 200
Indianapolis, IN 46204
www.ibjbp.com

The author has made every effort to ensure the accuracy of
the information within this book and to credit the sources
appropriately.

ISBN 978-1-939550-61-3
First Edition

Library of Congress Control Number: 2017941795

Printed in the United States of America

DEDICATION

I AM DEDICATING THE BOOK TO MY OLD MAN. Thomas A. Bowen has been there for me during the entire story. He gave me foreman opportunities, was an investor in Bowen Engineering, and he fed me Indiana construction news while I was in California. But most important he taught me great values.

My Dad was the nicest guy in town. I never heard him cuss, he didn't smoke and only drank an occasional beer. He treated people right. That has had a big impact on me and hopefully I will measure up to his standards.

ACKNOWLEDGEMENTS

First and foremost, I need to thank my family. They have been there for me every step of the way, starting with my sweetie, Terry Bowen, whom I married in 1989. If I had not married her, there would be no book. Actually, if she had married someone else, he would have written the book and not me. I have spent fifteen months and 1,200 man-hours writing *It Takes More Than Concrete*. She has been at my side the entire time as a sounding board, counsel, and the source of many very good suggestions. She came up with the tag "How to Build a Construction Business From the Ground Up."

Brian Stater is Terry's son and chief public works estimator for Bowen Engineering. His quotes and homespun expressions are interspersed throughout the book. Ain't life grand?

Kris Bowen got us into performance contracting. In 2017, performance contracting will be 35 percent of our annual business. Her husband and my son-in-law, Mark Bowell, gave me the idea for the book title, *It Takes More Than Concrete*.

Bowen Engineering's CEO and my son, Albert Douglas Bowen III, shows up throughout the book. His leadership and forward thinking are what makes everything work. I wrote the first fifty years of the company's history. It will be up to Doug to write the next fifty.

My employees have been critical in writing the book, but no one has had more impact than Jeff Purdue. His creativity and genuine concern for others are what Bowen Engineering is all about. He is a leader, teacher, rainmaker, but most importantly, he truly cares about people.

Senior management helped me write several episodes. I could not have written the chapters on Lean and regional offices without their leadership and creativity. They are:

- Aaron Purdue
- Bill Fyffe
- John Dettman
- Ed Storrs
- Matt Gentry

- Mark Cvetkovich
- Alan Dale
- Pat Meunier
- Pat Stanford
- Lacy Wargel

Several business associates outside the Bowen Family helped. They consulted with me, gave me suggestions, sometimes corrected my thinking, and generally confirmed the material. They are listed in chapter order.

- Al Oak, President, Cripe Engineering
- Hugh Rice, Sr. Chairman, FMI Corporation
- Gerald Lyles, Sr. Vice President, Lyles Diversified, Inc.
- Tom Shelby, Executive Vice President, Peter Kiewit and Sons
- Kyrk Reid, Peter Kiewit and Sons
- Bob Kula, Vice President/Communications, Peter Kiewit and Sons
- Bob Abel, Director in Charge, Blue & Co.
- Larry Steinberg, Sr. Manager, Blue & Co.
- Steve Coats, Managing Partner, International Leadership Assoc.
- Dan Suwyn, Partner, Workplace Dynamics
- Greg Howell, Chairman, Lean Construction Institute
- Michael Burns, Technical Writer/Editor, Construction Industry Institute
- Kevin Adams, Regional Underwriting Officer, Travelers Indemnity
- Richard Pepper, Executive, Pepper Construction
- Bill Dudley, CEO Retired, Bechtel Corporation

My family and Bowen employees reviewed and commented on the final draft. They are listed.

- Julie Bowen
- Stacy Stater
- Steve Nutt
- Scot Evans
- Tom Greve
- Mike Soller

Next, I must recognize Rahul Anand. Rahul is from India and was my student at Purdue in the fall of 2015. He earned an A+. At the end of the semester, he suggested that I write a book about small construction companies. He said there are no books available like that. At first, I passed his suggestion off as not being very realistic. I started writing the book in February of 2016.

Lisa Abbott is my editor and writing coach. She was provided by my publisher, Mickey Maurer. Lisa is talented, a hard worker, very creative, and has a wonderful attitude. But most importantly, she cares about me and the book. That is a big deal and it means a lot to me. The book is definitely improved because of her efforts.

Last, but not least, is Rinda Carey. Rinda has been my assistant for twenty-nine years. I don't know where we would be without Rinda. She certainly helped me keep the book organized and also chased down a bunch of references. I don't know how she found some of them. Rinda, you are my hero.

In the construction business, being successful takes much more than concrete. I've learned over the past year that writing a book also takes more than the author. I'm grateful to everyone who has played a part in the process of making the idea of this work a reality.

TABLE OF CONTENTS

FOREWORD

As you follow along with the journey of Bob Bowen throughout this book, you get a sense of what made the man and what made the business. It's a journey we celebrate everyday, and especially today, as we enter our fiftieth year of business at Bowen Engineering Corporation. But the personal stories and the shared lessons learned are timeless and invaluable, to budding engineers and students of business, as well as the most seasoned entrepreneur.

Personally, I never tire of the stories from his fifty-five-year career, because these are stories told by my father. It makes me so proud to witness the business that he and my mother started in 1967; to see the employees' lives changed, the communities improved, and the honest and hardworking quest to build a reputable business along the way.

Along with that quest, a unique esprit de corps has been created at Bowen Engineering. And in the pages that follow, you'll understand the genesis and evolution of that spirit. We work to keep it alive on a daily basis, thanks in large part to my father's vision and constant dedication to the process, and most importantly, to people. As we look to the future, we are sure we want to remain the leader in our marketplace, but it's our focus on people and enabling employees to become leaders that makes our business great. We are all in this together, and as I often say, "None of us is as smart as all of us." As you read along, it will become clear how I came up with that mentality. It's because I learned from the best.

Doug Bowen
CEO and President
Bowen Engineering Corporation

PROLOGUE

The seeds of this entire story were planted back in the nineteenth century. My great-grandfather Thomas Morse ran a commercial building business under the name of Morse Construction. His company worked on the original court house in Greensburg, Indiana, which is now famous for the tree growing out of its roof. When he died, the business was turned over to his son, Robert. The company did not survive. My grandmother, Ella Bowen, never forgave her brother for losing the family business.

Enter my grandfather, Albert D. Bowen Sr., who was married to Ella. Albert or A.D., as he was affectionately called, was a tailor. He and Ella had four boys: Morse, Albert D. Jr., Robert M., and Thomas A. (my father). In 1906, Robert was run over by a streetcar at the intersection of Fall Creek Boulevard and Central Avenue in Indianapolis. His leg was amputated on the kitchen table in the family home at 22nd Street and Broadway.

As a result of the accident, the family received a sizable settlement from the streetcar company. With the proceeds, A.D. started his own alley paving business and named it the A. D. Bowen Construction Company. He built most of the brick alleys in downtown Indianapolis in the early twentieth century and became known as the "Alley King."

When A.D. died in 1929, Robert took over the business. Robert realized that brick pavers were not the future, so he turned it into a concrete paving company and changed the name to R. M. Bowen

Construction. My dad joined the company in 1951. He was the first college graduate in the family and pretty much ran the business for the next twenty years, until it closed in 1972.

My dad was an outstanding project manager and superintendent. When uncle Robert died in 1970, it fell to my dad to run the business. He was not an entrepreneur and my mother realized that if my dad continued to run the business, they would go broke. So, the business was closed in 1972. It begs the question, why didn't I step in and help my dad? But I had my own company by this time and there is no way that I could have run two companies. It was never even a consideration.

I was brought up in a construction family. I was very fortunate. I worked for my dad in the summers while I went to Purdue. My dad was a good construction man and a really nice guy. My mother, a Goodwin from Washington, Indiana, was the tough one in the family. I picked up good qualities from both of my parents, but most importantly, I learned good values that served me well as I started and ran my own business.

I was not an outstanding youngster growing up. I almost flunked kindergarten. No one flunked kindergarten in 1945. I was 225th out of 625 in my high school graduating class. Even my high school geometry teacher told me that I would not make it through Purdue. My grandfather told my mother that I wouldn't amount to anything. With a 2.0 grade point average after two years at Purdue, I was pretty much on the way to proving them all correct.

The one saving grace for me was that I played alto saxophone in my cousin's dance band, "Tommy Wood Splinters." Tom and I had our own act in the Junior Vaudeville, the annual musical extravaganza at Shortridge High School. I've always believed that my high school music experience may have saved me. Wood's grandfather was my uncle, Robert M. Bowen, the one who lost his leg in the streetcar accident.

I was a good worker and construction fit right into my game plan. My dad had a joint venture partner, Vogel Construction. The owner, Harry Weaver, bragged on me as a worker (something I found out many years later). It's so important that kids learn to do something well as they grow up. Success builds on success.

I dropped out of Purdue after my sophomore year and worked for the Indiana State Highway Department for nine months. I ran a survey crew and was fairly good at it. They always gave me the tough assignments. Interestingly, I worked for Gene Halleck, who eventually became head of the highway department. His assistant was Bob Coma, who eventually ran Howard, Needles, Tammen and Bergandoff, a national engineering firm.

When I returned to Purdue in the fall of 1960, I had renewed objectives. I said, "I am not stupid, I can make A's." That next semester, I made straight A's. I actually made A's and B's from then on and raised my GPA to a 3.0 when I graduated. You learn more from your failures than your successes in life.

Front Row L-R: Morse Bowen, A. Douglas Bowen, Jr. (II)
Back Row L-R: Robert M. Bowen, Thomas A. Bowen (Bob Bowen's father)

When I graduated from Purdue, joining the family business was not an option. By raising my GPA, I was able to land a really great job with Kaweah Construction, a subsidiary of the W. M. Lyles Company in Visalia, California. I was certain that I had the greatest job of all time. I owned stock, traveled the state of California building projects, and bid many of my own jobs. How lucky was I? I look back on those times and treasure the experience. I have maintained a relationship with the Lyles family over the years. The family is the namesake of the Lyles School of Civil Engineering at Purdue.

There are chuck holes in the road of life, and I have certainly had mine. Those early life experiences are what shaped me into the man I have become. I had good values and I was a hard worker. Traveling away from home was good for me. It taught me self-reliance, confidence, and leadership. I think that all young people should get away from home as they venture out into the real world.

I started Bowen Engineering in 1967. We celebrate our fiftieth anniversary in 2017. In this book, I will attempt to discuss the things that have worked well and kept us alive. We will examine the changes we made along the way and the values that have defined our company. In 1967, there were twelve companies that built water and wastewater treatment plants in Indiana. Ours is the only company remaining in 2017. The others have all disappeared.

The objective of this book is an investment in the future generation of construction professionals. I have compiled the knowledge and experience gained over many years as a source of instruction and inspiration to students and entrepreneurs. Let's see how we started this wonderful business.

1

CALIFORNIA, HERE WE COME

*"To be successful in construction, you must pay attention to
detail and have genuine concern for others."*
–William E. Brown Jr., president retired,
Kaweah Construction

I never planned to start a construction business. When I left Purdue in 1962, it was not even on the radar. I am guessing the seed was planted because I had been brought up in a construction family. In California, I was bidding many of my own projects for Kaweah Construction and then managing those projects. I bid the Ojai Waste Water Treatment Plant, just north of Los Angeles, and then ran the project. I bid the Morro Bay Wastewater Treatment Plant, just north of San Luis Obispo, and then ran that job. We were low bidder on the Morro Bay project by $50,000. I remember that the owners did some investigation into Kaweah, to see if we were a reputable contractor. The report they got back was that they would not be able to hire a better company than Kaweah Construction. Whenever my family would travel, we would stop by some of my projects.

I don't remember ever losing money on any of my projects. Conversely, I don't remember ever beating budget. I was probably a better-than-average project manager but not a great project manager. I worked for Bill Brown, president of Kaweah Construction. He was a professional in every sense of the word. He was a brilliant engineer with a civil engineering degree from

Dartmouth and a master's degree in construction management from Stanford. He was smooth with owners, unions, and leaders in the industry. I have been successful in great degree because I have emulated Bill Brown. I love the man and treasure the time I spent with him.

Family travels - Bob and his daughter, Kris, in Weir Trough

One of my best examples of Brown and his high standards was on a job in Modesto, California. We were building a small concrete bridge as a sub for a paving contractor. I was project manager. The bridge had drilled concrete piling under the abutment piers. Our sub had bid $33,000 for the work and I had used that price in the bid. After the bidding, a late price came in at $30,000. I asked Bill if we should use the lower price. He said absolutely not. He said that if the sub wanted to submit a bid to Kaweah, they had to bid on time.

Kaweah was a subsidiary of Lyles Construction. Brown, with his own initiative and effort, took Kaweah into the water and wastewater treatment plant construction business. He had to learn the specialized bidding expertise and construction skills on his own. His creativity, even though I was not an employee at the time, is what led me into the water and wastewater business. Without that, I probably would never have gotten into the business myself. Water and wastewater construction is unique. In order to compete, you need to self-perform the concrete and the mechanical work. If you subcontract either of those disciplines, you have two markups—the subcontractor's and yours.

Lindsay Ripe Olive Depressed Railroad Siding

I will never forget my first day at Kaweah Construction in Visalia, California. I walked into the office and they were bidding a depressed railroad siding in Exeter, California. I helped on the bid. We were successful and I served as project engineer for the project. The site was in hardpan, so Brown decided to dig the hole neat and use the excavation as the back form.

Since we formed only one side of the walls, bracing was complicated. The walls on both sides of the pit were braced against each other. We then poured the walls simultaneously. We had to be careful not to overload either side, or the forms would move out of line.

Form system

Finished siding

Delta Mendota Canal Bridge Project

One of my most interesting and most important projects in California was the Delta Mendota Canal project in Firebaugh, California. We had to replace twenty-two bridges over the canal. Eighteen were farm bridges and four were pipe bridges. The rub was that the canal would only be out of operation for thirty days. In California, water is like gold. An additional complication was that work over canals was covered by the Pile Driver's Union, and the nearest union hall was in Los Angeles, 200 miles south of the project. We didn't have any full-time pile drivers, so the entire crew was out of the union hall.

Brown had bid the project and I was to be project manager. The superintendent was Vestel Harris, who had not been with Kaweah very long. The original bridges had timber piers and superstructures. The new bridges were to have precast concrete piers and treated timber superstructures. General consensus was that a contractor would purchase the concrete piers from a precast concrete manufacturer. But Brown, in his infinite wisdom, figured to manufacture the piers in our yard in Visalia. We built the piers by stacking them. This is the same method used in casting tilt up wall panels.

Casting piers - Brown is the tall guy on the right.

Setting piers - that's me on the far side of the canal.

Wood joists

We could do a lot of work before the canal was taken out of operation. We staged all materials, including the concrete piers, the creosoted timber, and the galvanized guard rail. We also dismantled the timber decks on the bridges, above the water line.

Harris and I were not working very well together. He didn't have a lot of urgency and didn't follow through with our plans. I am sure that he was not happy with me, either. He probably thought I was interfering with his management of the project. You can't blame Vestel. He was a thirty-year veteran in construction and I was a twenty-five-year-old rookie engineer. The day before the canal was to be taken out of service, Harris quit.

I knew in a New York-second who was going to run the job. I called Brown and told him Vestel had quit and that I was going to run the job. I had been in the field for three years and thought I could do it. Now, instead of having to coerce Harris into doing his job, I could take care of business. I showed up at the jobsite on Monday morning at 6:30 and the pile drivers were all there. I told the crew that Harris had quit and that I was now superintendent. At Kaweah, we planned three days ahead, so we had a plan and simply went to work. Naturally, I was nervous, but the next thing I knew, it was five o'clock and the day was done.

I set up five crews: a demo crew, a pier crew, a deck crew, a pipe crew, and a miscellaneous crew. The union agreement required one foreman, so we had only one foreman. That was a mistake. We should have had five foremen. We had lead men on each crew and that was the plan. One further complication was that the canal was so flat that it would not drain. We had to have a dry canal to install the piers. So, we had to build a dam at the downstream end of our work zone and pump the canal dry. I designed a pump structure with some really big pumps and we drained the canal.

We finished the job on time and made a small profit. We did not beat budget. Brown was not happy with my performance. He felt, and rightly so, that I was a micro-manager. He gave me a serious dressing down at the end of the project, for which I am still smarting. I made some mistakes. I should certainly have had more foremen. But I learned that I could run a job. I think that the experience was invaluable as I started my new company.

As I reminisce about the day Harris quit, I wonder why I didn't call for a replacement superintendent. I am curious as to why Brown didn't step in. He could have fired me. I suspect that was what Harris hoped would happen. I also suspect that Harris thought we could not build the job without him.

Finished farm bridge with Bob Bowen - 40 years later

Exploring the Idea of Business Ownership

I was brought up in the construction business and I was a reasonably good estimator. I had management experience in the field and I knew the water and wastewater business. I think that it was a natural flow of events that led me to consider starting my own company. I thought I could run my own company. So, in 1965, I actually met with my dad's lawyer, bonding agent, and accountant, back in Indianapolis. My dad had been sending me construction reports and bid letting results on water and wastewater projects in Indiana. We decided to start the new company in 1966. I would be twenty-six years old.

But when 1966 rolled around, the economy was in the dumpster, which it always is, and I chickened out. I remember contacting all of my experts back in Indianapolis and telling them that I had decided to cancel the new company for the time being.

About that time, my relationship with Brown started to develop some stress. He was simply not happy with my performance. He thought that I was a micro-manager. He felt that I was doing everything myself and not delegating effectively. I thought, "Give me a break!" No one was as smart as I was. I was a left-brained engineer and I didn't trust anyone else to do my work.

Brown and I had planned a meeting in the main office, I think, to discuss my performance. When the date arrived, we were pretty busy at my project site. We were setting 108-inch diameter concrete pipe with a 65-ton rental crane on concrete cradles 40 feet below grade. It was a critical and complicated operation, so I cancelled the meeting.

He caught up with me that afternoon and naturally wanted to know why I had cancelled the meeting. He then asked me to come to the main office, which was about an hour away. He asked me if I had anything else planned. I knew this was it for old Bob, and that I was going to get canned. So, I walked into his office and quit. As it turned out, he wasn't going to fire me. We agreed that I would finish the San Luis Canal project, which was six months from completion. Essentially, I gave him six months' notice. I called my dad and told him that I had quit.

I felt so badly about leaving Brown that I retracted my resignation the next day. He said no, I should leave at the end of the San Luis project. I had six months to finish the work and plan the rest of my life.

Opportunities Back Home, in Indiana

I decided to get a job in Indiana, learn the lay of the land, and then start my own business. I contacted five construction companies who were building water and wastewater treatment projects in Indiana. I had a pretty good resume. I was a registered professional engineer in California and I had estimated and built some pretty neat projects.

Most of the companies were interested in talking to me when I returned to Indiana. Acton Construction set up an interview for me at their main office in Minneapolis. They were building the Lafayette Wastewater Treatment Plant. The company I was most interested in was C & C Construction out of Ft. Wayne, Indiana. They were the largest of the group. William Curtis, their president, sent me a letter asking for references and salary requirements. I replied and used Brown as my only reference. I asked for five dollars per hour, which was carpenter's pay.

3417 East Simpson
Fresno, Ca. 93703
May 7, 1967

Evans Construction Co.
R. R. 1, Box 145
Westfield, Indiana

Gentlemen:

Upon completion of the construction project on
which I am currently engaged I plan to leave my present
employer and move to the Midwest. I am writing this
letter in quest of employment with your firm.

At the present time I am project manager on a $500,000
pumping plant. I am looking for a similar type position
and should be available for work on September 1, 1967.
My qualifications are as follows:

Experience: Five years with a general engineering contractor in California, specializing in sewage
treatment plants and bridge construction.
Two of those years in the capacity of project
engineer and three years as project manager.
My work has covered all phases of construction including estimating, supervision over
labor and equipment, project planning and
scheduling, production control, material
purchasing, cost analysis, and customer
billing.

Engineering: Registered Civil Engineer in the state of
California holding Certificate No. 17092.

Education: B. S. Degree in Civil Engineering from
Purdue University.

Age: 27 years old.

Family: Wife and five year old daughter.

I am prepared to move as the job demands and I realize
that we don't keep banker's hours in the construction
industry. If you are interested or have any questions,
please advise.

Very truly yours,

Robert L. Bowen

Evans employment letter

I never heard back from C & C. I didn't figure that Brown would give me a bad reference, so I assumed that I had asked for too much money. In California, I had been the project manager, working 24/7's, bidding the work, and managing the projects, and I made less than the journeyman carpenters. It sounded like the same deal in Indiana. I said, "I can starve on my own. I don't need C & C." That was when I decided to launch Bowen Engineering. I called Roger Acton in Minneapolis and cancelled the interview. I told him that I was starting my own company. He asked me what the name of the company would be and I said, "Bowen Engineering." He said they would be looking out for Bowen Engineering. And that was the beginning. Acton eventually went out of business. Acton became a facilitator for Total Quality Management. He even did a project for Bowen Engineering. He didn't remember me. Interestingly, I ran into Curtis a few years later and mentioned the letter I had sent him. He said that it had been lost and he actually would liked to have hired me.

The Final Chapter with Kaweah

My last assignment for Kaweah was on the San Luis Canal. It was comprised of three different projects. One was concrete lift stations for Kiewit Construction and the other two were concrete structures on two pipe line distribution projects for Granite Construction in Watsonville, California and Beasley Engineering in Oakland, California. I thought that Beasley Engineering was a neat name and that is how I arrived at the name Bowen Engineering. I got to know the project manager at Kiewit. I told him that I was leaving Kaweah at the end of the project. He said that Kaweah would miss me. That compliment has stuck with me all these years. Mark Twain said, "A good compliment will last me two months." That one has lasted fifty years.

I served as project manager for three years at Kaweah. I only had one project engineer and that was on the San Luis Canal. The project engineer was Gerald Lyles, the owner's son. He was a typical Lyles; very sharp. I consider it an honor to have been his boss for that short period.

I owned Kaweah stock, which I had purchased for $7,500, and cashed out for $15,000. The stock was financed by the Lyles Family. Mrs. Lyles told me that I paid off the loan quicker than any previous employee. I also had $15,000 in the stock market. I put everything I had into the new company. My dad also invested $15,000, for a total of $45,000.

I didn't own a home in California. A fellow project manager at Lyles had told me to rent. If you own a home, he said, you are tied down and lose flexibility. If I had owned a home, I could not have moved to Ojai, Morro Bay, or Fresno. I also saved money. That savings helped me start my business.

Interestingly, three months before I was to leave Kaweah, Brown asked me to stay with Kaweah, after all. I told him that I planned to start my own company in Indiana. As I look back, I realize that was an opportunity for me to chicken out again. But honestly, it never crossed my mind. I guess I was destined to start Bowen Engineering.

I think that starting a new company has to be natural flow of events. You have to go with the flow. The pieces and parts fell into place for me. Everything seemed to be guiding me towards Bowen Engineering. Starting a new business that is completely divorced from your experience is dangerous and probably a mistake.

Lessons Learned

- Everyone should take control of their lives. You don't want others making life decisions for you. That is true for business and personal life.
- Starting a business has to be a natural flow. Changing direction by 90 or 180 degrees is difficult and dangerous.
- When starting a new business, you must have some expertise in the business.
- To be in construction, you must have good values.

2

BUSINESS PLAN

"Entrepreneurship is a grand game and money is simply a means of keeping score. The essence of entrepreneurship is the joy of the game."
–Mickey Maurer, Maurer School of Law, Indiana University, and chairman, IBJ Media

A business plan is an analysis of a business venture. It includes strategy, assumptions, and financial projections. It serves as a guide for management and as a prospectus for potential investors. In our case, we were not looking for investors. When I started our company, I did not have a formal business plan. But I had a plan. I had to, in order to obtain performance and payment bonds and a bank credit line. What follows is what our business plan would have looked like in 1967. Everything in the plan is what I actually thought about as I started our company.

When you are starting a new business it is critical that a few people believe in you. In my case it was my dad, my wife, the bank and the bonding company. Absent that support, I don't think I would have been successful. In starting a company you will have to sell yourself, and your plan. For the company to survive, you will have to continue to work your plan.

BOWEN ENGINEERING CORPORATION

Mission/Vision

Be the best water and wastewater treatment plant contractor in the Midwest. Develop the best team of construction workers in the business, who will love working for Bowen Engineering Corporation.

Executive Summary

The company will build water and wastewater treatment plants in Indiana. Robert L. Bowen will be president and CEO. He just completed six years of similar construction with the W. M. Lyles Company in Fresno, California. While there, he traveled the state, bidding and managing his own projects. He was a stockholder with the Lyles Company and is a registered civil engineer in the state of California.

Our competition will be contractors who also self-perform the work, however there is a limited number of available contractors. General and mechanical contractors have a difficult time competing in this market because they don't provide both disciplines and must subcontract a major portion of the work.

Our target market will be public and private water and wastewater treatment plants. We will have to be low bidder. We will not have a marketing department, but our president will make marketing/sales calls with prospective private owners. We will have to demonstrate that we can perform the work and provide prospective owners with suitable financial information and performance and payment bonds. Naturally, owners will want to know that we have the skill to perform the work. To demonstrate that we have these skills, we will rely on Mr. Bowen's experience from California.

Our goal is to pick up two projects the first year, putting $300,000 in place and returning 5 percent EBITDA (net profit). We will start with a $45,000 investment and augment that with a $50,000 credit line at Merchants National Bank.

The Company

Corporate Officers:
- Robert L. Bowen, president
- Judy H. Bowen, secretary

- Thomas A. Bowen, director
- Annalee Bowen, director

While I (Bob Bowen) was working in California, I bid much of my own work and then served as project manager on the projects that we won. I don't remember ever losing money on a project. I will bring that previous success and my skills to the new company.

Quality, value, and respect for the individual will be bywords at Bowen Engineering. We plan to hire future managers and engineers from the college ranks. We plan to sell stock to our most promising superintendents and project managers. If our young leaders are going to bank their lives and careers on Bowen, the least we can do is share our rewards with those individuals. Our employees will love working at Bowen Engineering.

Long term, we plan to expand outside the state of Indiana. We will build a reputation for quality and value. Our employees will be part of the family and will someday retire from Bowen with nice pensions and a feeling of success. We hope to hand the company to the next generation of leaders.

Product/Service

Our product is building water and wastewater treatment plants throughout the state of Indiana. We will be a self-perform construction company, doing the concrete construction, mechanical construction, and earthwork ourselves. By doing so, we will eliminate double markups on subcontractors and provide a more competitive price.

The water and wastewater industry is unique. The barriers to entry are challenging, in that there are not many contractors that can self-perform multi-trades. The industry is not fast growing, but it is steady because society is growing.

Market

Our target market will be public and private water and wastewater treatment plants throughout the state of Indiana. We can build new plants from the ground up or we can refurbish and expand existing plants.

The market is not fast growing, but it is steady. There are new projects out for bid every day in the *Construction News*. The market is typically seeing three to five bidders on a water or wastewater project, as compared to seven to fifteen bidders on a building project. As a result, water and wastewater contractors are seeing on average 4 to 5 percent net profit, compared to 1 to 2 percent on a building project. On the other hand, there is more risk on a wastewater project. The building contractors can lay much of their risk off on their subcontractors.

There is little respect or appreciation for value-added or quality construction. It is a low-price business. Contractors are a commodity. Everything is per plans and specs. However, it is not all gloom and doom. Many public works owners, design engineers, and quality contractors have very good relationships and are creating contract deliveries that include teamwork and partnering.

Owners are experiencing excessive claims. They are gun shy and searching for ways of eliminating and/or reducing claims. There is an opportunity for quality-minded contractors to work with owners and to build projects successfully.

Competition

There currently are eleven companies building water and wastewater treatment plants in Indiana. We have identified who we think are the most important players:

- Acton Construction, Minneapolis, Minnesota
- C & C Construction, Ft. Wayne, Indiana
- Shamrock Construction, Michigan City, Indiana
- AVCO Construction, Indianapolis, Indiana
- Evans Construction, Carmel, Indiana

Acton and C & C are pretty big and probably outside the scope of what we are attempting. The two toughest competitors, in our weight class, will be Evans and AVCO. Both are highly respected and have great relationships in the industry. The good news is that they raise the quality of the bidding and the construction process. Their market presence gives quality contractors an opportunity to win a good job at a fair price and not suffer from low-ball pricing, which ruins projects for everyone.

Today, most general contractors are brokers. They subcontract most of the project. Any work that is being subcontracted has two markups; one for the sub and one for the general contractor. We believe that the general and mechanical contractors will not be competitive in this industry sector. The biggest general contractor in the area is Wilhelm Construction and the biggest mechanical contractor is BMW. Both are excellent contractors, but they have the inherent disadvantage of having to subcontract a major portion of the project. Therefore, we are not considering them to be a factor.

Sales and Marketing

Our target is the water and wastewater market. The first step is to find out about future projects being bid. Most projects are reported in the local *Construction News,* a daily newspaper dedicated to the construction industry. The publication reports the project description, the size of the project, and bid date.

Some water and wastewater treatment plants will be built by private owners. These owners will also report their projects in the *Construction News,* but bidding on these projects will be by invitation only. The only way we can get on the bid list of those private owners is to build a solid reputation. The president will make marketing and sales calls and network with private owners. This emphasizes the importance of doing a really good job on our first projects. Word of mouth is going to be an important selling tool.

We are going to be active in the community and in the construction industry. We will participate in the National Society of Professional Engineers and the American Society of Civil Engineers. We will join the Associated General Contractors of America, the elite group of general contractors. If we associate with the best contractors in the industry, hopefully, people will think of us as one of the best. This should get our name out in the public and put us in touch with industry leaders.

Membership and participation in the local Chamber of Commerce is also in our game plan. Here we can network with local businessmen and develop relationships for the future.

Operations

Cash is king, and we will have to husband our cash reserves. To save office expenses, our first office will be in the residence of our president. This means there will be no receptionist and phone calls will be handled by a local answering service. Our $45,000 investment will have to carry us until we get our first project.

In the early days, our president will be chief cook and bottle washer. He must find work, bid the work, manage the projects, do payroll and accounts payable, secure necessary insurance, and sweep the floor. His pay will be deferred until we receive our first cash receipts.

Our workforce will come from the local trade unions. By joining the trade unions, we get quality trained journeymen wherever we travel. We will pay a fair day's pay for a fair day's work. And we don't have to carry a workforce if the work runs out. To hire superintendents and foremen, we will ask the union business agents to recommend qualified and experienced leaders. We will then interview candidates and hire accordingly. Each foreman and superintendent will be provided a company pickup truck for travel to and from work.

Since we must husband our cash, we plan to rent heavy equipment on an as-needed basis. In the future, we will own our fleet of heavy equipment. By owning our equipment, we think we can provide a more competitive price.

Financial

Our initial investment will be $45,000. The amount will include $30,000 from Robert L. Bowen and $15,000 from his father, Thomas A. Bowen, who will not be involved in the day-to-day running of the business. We expect to put $300,000 in place during the first year, with an Earnings Before Interest, Taxes, Debt Service, and Amortization (EBITDA) of 5 percent. Our break-even amount is $175,000 the first year. Pro-forma (Fig. 1) and break-even analysis (Fig. 2) are attached.

We have met with Merchants National Bank and they have agreed to provide a $50,000 credit line to augment our cash needs. Seaboard Surety will provide performance and payment bonds for our public works construction. They will bond us up to a $400,000 work program. The construction industry standard revenue/equity ratio is ten. We are at 8.9, which we think is excellent, given that we have not completed any work as a firm. The bank has requested a cash flow analysis (Fig. 3).

BOWEN ENGINEERING - PRO FORMA					
SUB "S" CORPORATION					
1967	1968	1969	1970	1971	1972
Income Statement					
Revenue	300,000	400,000	600,000	1,000,000	1,500,000
Growth %		33.3%	50.0%	66.7%	50.0%
Direct Costs (COG)	264,000	352,000	534,000	900,000	1,350,000
Gross Profit	36,000	48,000	66,000	100,000	150,000
Gross Profit (%/rev)	12.0%	12.0%	11.0%	10.0%	10.0%
Overhead (G & S) Sheet 2	21,000	25,000	35,000	58,000	84,000
Overhead (G & A) %	8.0%	7.1%	6.6%	6.4%	6.2%
Total Cost	285,000	377,000	569,000	958,000	1,434,000
EBITDA (net profit)	15,000	23,000	31,000	42,000	66,000
EBITDA as % of revenue	5.0%	5.8%	5.2%	4.2%	4.4%
Taxes (25%)	3,750	5,750	7,750	10,500	16,500
Profit After Tax	11,250	17,250	23,250	31,500	49,500
Financial Analysis					
Equity	45,000	56,250	73,500	96,750	128,250	177,750
Turns On Equity		6.3	6.7	7.7	9.9	11.2
Total Company Shares	4,500	4,500	4,500	4,500	4,500	4,500
Value Per Share (Par)	10.00	12.50	16.33	21.50	28.50	39.50
Net Return on Equity		25.0%	30.7%	31.6%	32.6%	38.6%
Earnings/Share		2.50	3.83	5.17	7.00	11.00

Fig. 1 Pro-forma

	BOWEN ENGINEERING		
	BREAK EVEN ANALYSIS		
	Gross margin = Revenue x 12%		
	Gross margin = Net profit + Overhead		
	Revenue x 12% = Net profit + Overhead		
	In a break even analysis Net Profit equals "0"		
	Rev (Brk Even) x 12% = Overhead		
	Rev (Brk Even) =	Overhead	
		12%	
	Rev (Brk Even) =	21,000	
		0.12	
	Rev (Brk Even) =	175,000	

Fig. 2 Break-even analysis

BOWEN ENGINEERING CORPORATION

CASH FLOW ANALYSIS

Description	Basis	Extension	Oct '67	Nov '67	Dec '67	Jan '68	Feb '68	Mar '68	April '68	May '68	June '68	July '68	Aug '68	Sep '68	Totals
Beginning Cash Balance			45,000	40,000	35,000	30,000	25,000	16,000	8,600	6,800	3,400	800	3,400	7,200	7,200
Project 1															
Contract		200,000													
Material	25%	50,000							6,000	6,000	6,000	12,000	12,000	6,000	50,000
Subs	25%	50,000							6,000	4,000	6,000	10,000	12,000	14,000	50,000
Labor	25%	50,000					4,000		8,000	10,000	8,000	4,000	4,000	4,000	50,000
Revenue	90%	180,000						9,600	19,200	21,600	26,400	36,000	33,600	28,800	175,200
Project 2															
Contract		200,000													
Material	25%	50,000										2,000	6,000	6,000	14,000
Subs	25%	50,000										2,000	2,000	4,000	8,000
Labor	25%	50,000									4,000	8,000	8,000	10,000	30,000
Revenue	90%	180,000										9,600	19,200	21,600	50,400
Net Cash Available							(4,000)	(2,400)	3,200	1,600	2,400	7,600	8,800	6,400	
Operating Expenses	8%	60,000	5,000	5,000	5,000	5,000	5,000	5,000	5,000	5,000	5,000	5,000	5,000	5,000	60,000
Ending Cash Balance			40,000	35,000	30,000	25,000	16,000	8,600	6,800	3,400	800	3,400	7,200	8,600	

Fig. 3 Cash flow analysis

Our first-year volume is projected to be $300,000. We are expecting to pick up two $200,000 contracts. We hope to complete one and be 50 percent complete on the other.

We expect to grow at a rate of approximately 50 percent per year. This may appear optimistic. We feel that once we get our forces in place and our reputation established, we can be somewhat aggressive on growth.

Average metrics over the initial five-year period:

- Gross margin – 11 percent
- Overhead as a percentage of direct costs – 6.5 percent trending to 5 percent.
- EBITDA (net profit)– 5 percent
- Turns on equity – 7.7
- Return on equity – 31 percent

Lessons Learned

- If you plan to start a business, you need a business plan.
- A marketing plan is critical.
- A startup company should have some competitive market advantage. What can you do better than the competition?

3

BOWEN ENGINEERING

"We want to do business with people who have the same values that we have."
– Albert Douglas Bowen III, president and CEO, Bowen Engineering Corporation

We had a new company and $45,000 in the bank. We didn't have an office, superintendent, construction workers, construction equipment, construction yard, or any work. The first thing we had to do was get incorporated and registered with the Secretary of State in Indiana. The State of Indiana didn't like our name. They contended that we were representing ourselves as engineers, but that I was not registered in Indiana. We got around it by the fact that my dad was registered and I was in the process of getting my Indiana license by reciprocity. We were officially incorporated on September 5, 1967.

I actually wrote down a set of company objectives and plans in 1967. My dad saved them and my daughter discovered them searching through old files. Here they are verbatim. It is interesting to note that our plans and objectives haven't changed much over fifty years.

Company Objectives

- Build a sound reputation with our customers and the community.
- Show 20 percent return on our investment each year.

Company Plans

- Workmanship must be top quality.
- Projects to be run with engineering guidance such as CPM, etc.
- Management will take part in local professional organizations such as NSPE & AGC.
- Equipment will be maintained in first-class condition, including the painting of trucks with the company colors (yellow and black).
- Reinvest profits in company.
- Make an attempt to finance large pieces of equipment such as pickup trucks, if we can obtain for 7.5 percent or less.
- Keep project cost accounting current at all times (recaps).
- Until company is in the black, salaries and any other monetary compensation will be kept at a minimum.
- Board of directors to share actively in the bidding and supervision of projects.
- Maintain an office unless the size of an individual project warrants moving it to the jobsite.
- Foremen will not be kept on between jobs.
- Responsible foremen will be furnished with a pickup while running the project.

The company was going to focus on water and wastewater treatment plant construction, which would be in the public works market. To do that, we would need a bonding company to underwrite our bids and performance. I met with George Dodd at Baldwin and Lyons, an agent for Seaboard Surety. Seaboard was probably the Cadillac of the industry in 1967. He told me, "This is not a crap shoot." He was impressed that at twenty-seven years old, I had saved $30,000 to put into the business. To support my request for bonds, I used references from the town manager in Morro Bay, California, and the design engineers on the Ojai and Morro Bay projects. Dodd agreed to bond a work program of up to $400,000 per year.

Setting Up Shop

My first office was the living room of my townhouse at 10th Street and Arlington in Indianapolis. I met suppliers, salesmen, and even my bonding company in the new office. If we had guests over for dinner, I threw everything into a closet and set up the dining room table for dinner. I had to husband that $45,000 and I was not going to waste good cash on a fancy office.

We did not have any work, so naturally, the company was not bringing in any revenue. In order to preserve my cash, I didn't draw a salary. My wife was a teacher, so we lived off of her income. We picked our home location because it was within walking distance of the grade school where she taught. I could then use the family car to run the business. When we got our first payment on our first job, I paid myself retroactively. What do you think I paid myself? Carpenters' wages. Five dollars per hour. I felt the company had to pay me or I couldn't afford to be in business. To start a new business, you must separate your company finances from your personal finances. I did that from the very beginning. You can't co-mingle the finances.

My outside accountant was a Big 8 firm. A year later, not being too happy with them, I changed to my dad's firm, Mott and Crane. Jack Crane was a new partner there and I was his first customer.

I needed operating capital. I met with my dad's bank, Merchants National Bank. Uncle Morse Bowen had been a senior vice president there. My loan officer was Kelsa Cook and he set up a credit line of $50,000. Unfortunately, Cook died almost a year later, at forty-seven years old. The bank moved my account to a branch on the north side of Indianapolis. The branch manager sat me down and explained that when they loaned me money, I would have to pay them back. Duh! Crane helped me find a new bank, American Fletcher National Bank (AFNB). Thanks, Jack.

The First Year in Business

Now we needed to find work. I needed to bid some jobs. Our first bid was a wastewater treatment plant expansion in Hanover, Indiana. How to mark it up? I didn't know what things cost in Indiana. I thought that markup should be 25 percent for general conditions, overhead, and profit. So, to be safe, I bid 35 percent on the first job, to see how we would do. We put in a pretty good bid. We were not the low bidder, but it confirmed to me that 25 percent was probably the right number.

Hanover Bid Results
- Munich Engineering Corp. $199,858
- Mitchell & Stark Construction Co.   218,408
- Bowen Engineering, Inc.   234,300
- Smith-Reed   256,350
- Edgar H. Hughes Co.   257,929

Our first low bid was a new wastewater treatment plant in Brookston, Indiana. The design engineer was Clark, Dietz and Associates out of Illinois, with an office in Lafayette. Their manager was David Hawkins, who remained friends with me until he died in 2000. Our bid was $180,000 and since we were the only bidder, we won the job.

Now, we had to go to work. We needed a project superintendent. What to do? I had been brought up in a union family and my California experience was in a union shop. I called the Carpenters Union in Lafayette for help. They recommended three journeyman carpenters with foreman experience. I set up shop in a motel in Lafayette and conducted interviews. We hired Elmer Benner to be our first project superintendent. For workers, I signed my first union agreements with the building trades in Lafayette. We were in business.

For construction equipment, I rented my dad's Lima 34 Crawler Crane and for small excavation, I rented small, rubber-tired backhoes from local excavators. We eventually bought the crane from my dad. We had to excavate a race track aeration tank. I rented two rubber-tired scrapers and hired operating engineers from the union. We got the job done. The aeration tank had 45-degree concrete slopes, which makes concrete placement very difficult. I had experience with sloped concrete in California. I designed special screed rails and hired my dad's concrete crews to place the concrete. They did a great job and the concrete was a success.

To run the job, we set up a $50,000 credit line at Merchants National Bank. To secure the credit line, the bank asked for a cash flow analysis. I had never done a cash flow analysis, but necessity is the mother of invention. We found the actual cash flow diagram for the Brookston job in the archives (Fig. 1). You can see that I expected to get paid net 15. Probably not too realistic.

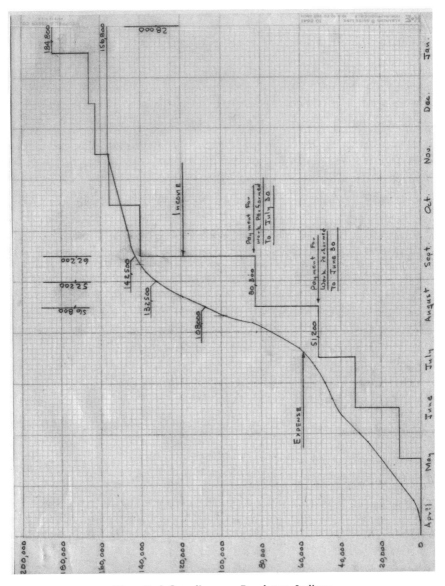

Fig. 1 Cash flow diagram - Brookston, Indiana

This all sounds good. But honestly, that first year was a nightmare. I didn't know if we would make any money and I didn't know if we could survive as a company. Superintendent Benner was driving a half-ton pickup truck. I had decided to put him in a three-quarter-ton truck. I asked my wife to travel to Lafayette and bring the half-ton truck back to Indianapolis. She took my daughter, Kris, and traveled to Lafayette on the train. On the way home, reaching for her purse, she lost control and rolled the vehicle. Kris had a broken collar bone and my wife had a lot of bruises. It is a miracle that they were not killed. My business insurance company refused to pay medical costs because they said that my wife was not on the payroll. My personal insurance refused to pay for medical costs because they said she was working. I fired both companies. The accident did not help my stress level.

After one year in business, I was a nervous wreck. I thought that if year two was no better, I had to get out of the business. We finished the Brookston job in November 1968, fourteen months after starting the company. We made $6,000 net profit after all expenses, including my retroactive pay. We had made a profit, and by this time we had picked up some more work. I felt pretty confident that we were going to make it, and the stress disappeared.

Brookston plaque

The Early Years

Our second job was in Jamestown, Indiana. Our bid was $120,000, but we were second bidder. The low bidder was at $100,000. He had made a bid mistake and withdrew his bid, making us the low bidder. We were over budget and the owner did not have enough funds for the project, so they asked us to extend our bid. I complied and asked for a $20,000 escalator. They met the price and we went to work. I met Bob Newman on that project. He worked for the sewer contractor who was also working for Jamestown. We hired his firm to do some excavation for us. The design engineer was Butler, Fairman and Seufert, out of Indianapolis. Our two firms are still doing design-build projects together fifty years later.

About 1970, things were starting to roll. We had picked up some jobs and then we won the Greensburg, Indiana Wastewater Treatment Plant Expansion. Our price was $440,000, and the second bidder was $480,000. We were almost 10 percent low. This was our largest contract to date. We purchased our American 399 crawler crane for that job. I thought Bowen Engineering had arrived. That crane is now on display at our Indianapolis office.

Then we had the opportunity to bid the Clinton, Indiana Wastewater Treatment Plan Expansion. The engineer's estimate was $700,000. It looked like we might be the only bidder. Dick Peterson, the Seaboard agent in Indiana, called and said that Seaboard would not provide a performance bond for the job. Seaboard was worried about Greensburg and thought that the Clinton job would over extend our financial resources. I said, "Dick, they have to bond the job. We will be the only bidder." He said his hands were tied, but that I could call New York. He gave me the name of the head of the Seaboard Bond Department, George Holbrook.

I called Holbrook. I had prepared a list of the reasons that Seaboard should bond the job on an 8.5 x 11 sheet of paper, single spaced. Two of the reasons were: 1) we planned to subcontract the mechanical portion to Shambaugh Mechanical out of Ft. Wayne, Indiana, and 2) we would be the only bidder. I convinced him and he agreed to bond the job.

We were the low and only bidder and our price was $900,000. The process equipment pricing had come in above our initial guestimate.

I was literally bouncing off the walls I was so excited. I called Holbrook the next morning to share our excitement and to thank him for the bond.

In the meantime, Holbrook had found out that our price was $900,000 when I had told him it would be $700,000. He thought he had been snookered. He was a bald-headed guy and he told me later that he was "red necked" when he heard the bid results.

So who was on the phone? The guy Holbrook personally wants to shoot. I explained what had happened. He bought it and provided the performance bond. Holbrook has since retired and we had lunch in Philadelphia in 2012.

We sit back and laugh at what is a great story. But what would have happened if I hadn't made that call the next morning? There is a better-than-even chance that Seaboard would not have provided our performance bond. And they would have had justification. We probably would have been unable to get a bond from another surety. We provided a 5 percent bid bond with our bid. If we had not gotten a performance bond, we would have had to forfeit the bid bond. That would have cost Bowen Engineering $45,000. Oops!

Lesson learned: don't forget to say thank you.

Fifty Years Later, What Stands Out

As I look back at those tumultuous times, the one thing that stands out is that I wanted my employees to love working at Bowen Engineering. I knew that if they were happy, they would give me their best effort. If they gave me their best effort, we would have our best chance of success.

Lessons Learned

Here are the basic values that I believed in when I started Bowen Engineering. If you are going to start a new business, these are good values to live by:

- Know the industry. Experience is vital.
- Cash is king.
  - No fancy offices.
  - No big salaries for the owner.
  - Rent construction equipment.
  - Husband your cash.

- Take good care of your employees.
  - They are your most important asset.
  - They must love working with your firm.
- You must know what it costs you to provide your service.
  - How much does it cost to operate a backhoe for an hour?
  - How much does it cost to erect a concrete form?
  - How much does it cost to pour a cubic yard of concrete?
- Have a marketing plan. It might be hard bid, but have a plan.
- Keep your business at arms-length. Treat it like a business, not your own personal expense account.
- Make a net profit on the first job.

4

ESTIMATING

"The first tenant of successful contracting is 'Get work at the right price.'"
-Peter Kiewit, Peter Kiewit and Sons

This quote was first used in the Kiewit Superintendents Manual in 1955. I guess it has stood the test of time. You have to price the work correctly and make a profit. You need to make a profit not because you are greedy, but because profit is the sustainer of the business and the measure of your success. It is the first place a bonding company, the bank, and owners will look to see if you know what you are doing. You have to make a profit on the first job. Loss leaders don't get much traction with me.

What does it take to be a good estimator? You have to be thorough and organized. College graduates in the schools of construction, construction engineering, and civil engineering are well suited for estimating because the rigorous education trains them to be thorough. You should have field experience because you have to know how to build something. Learn to double-check your estimates. For example, when I estimate an operation by man-days or man-hours, I double-check my estimate by calculating the unit price generated. If my unit price seems wrong, I relook at the estimate. When the big companies enter a joint venture, both companies estimate the same work. This approach helps them avoid major mistakes and omissions. On a $1 billion project, a $50 million mistake could be a problem.

There is a difference between estimating and bidding. Estimating is the mechanics of pricing the job. Bidding is the strategy and management of that estimate. What price are you going to give to the owner? We will discuss the mechanics of estimating in the first part of this chapter and then close with a discussion of bidding strategy.

I learned to estimate from Bill Brown at Kaweah Construction. Brown was a very good estimator. He told W. M. Lyles, his boss, that I estimated the work just like he did. That stuck with me. My advice to young estimators is to estimate just like your boss. Don't reinvent the wheel until you are the boss.

Direct Cost Summary

You have to be organized in the estimating process. The biggest danger to any estimate is leaving something out of the bid. At Bowen Engineering, we use the Construction Specification Institute's sixteen divisions (Fig. 1). For us, the major divisions are site work, concrete, mechanical, and process equipment. On larger jobs, each of those divisions is assigned to a specific estimator. The same person will usually do the concrete on all of our jobs. They then estimate the labor, equipment, materials, and subcontractors and enter the total onto the Direct Cost Summary. At Bowen, the direct cost summary is on green paper. We call it the green sheet. This summary is done manually, rather than on Microsoft® Excel. It is made available to everyone working on the bid.

BOWEN ENGINEERING

DIRECT COST SUMMARY

SPEC DIVISION	DESCRIPTION	LABOR	EQUIPMENT	MATERIALS	SUBS	TOTALS
1	GENERAL CONDITIONS					
2	SITEWORK					
3	CONCRETE					
4	MASONRY					
5	METALS					
6	WOOD AND PLASTICS					
7	THERMAL/MOISTURE PROTECTION					
8	DOORS AND WINDOWS					
9	FINISHES					
10	SPECIALTIES					
11	EQUIPMENT					
12	FURNISHINGS					
13	SPECIAL CONSTRUCTION					
14	CONVEYING SYSTEMS					
15	MECHANICAL					
16	ELECTRICAL					
	TOTAL DIRECT COST					
	(Transfer to Bid Pricing Sheet)					

Fig. 1 Direct cost summary

Bid Pricing Sheet

The bid pricing sheet is done on an Excel spreadsheet and includes total direct costs, general conditions, overhead, and contract profit (Fig. 2). We use this sheet to develop our final price to the owner. In the old days, the construction company owner went into the back room to apply overhead and profit. Companies don't do that today, I hope. It is a collaborative effort. Everyone working on the bid has a voice. We try to have the direct cost summary completed at least twenty-four hours before the bid letting.

		BOWEN ENGINEERING			
PROJECT:		BID PRICING SHEET			
DUE DATE:		INCLUDES GENERAL CONDITIONS, OVERHEAD & MARKUP			
DESCRIPTION	LABOR	EQUIPMENT	MAT'LS	SUBS	TOTAL
Summary of Direct Costs		(From Direct Cost Summary)			
Change Sheets					
Total Direct Cost					
Supervision					
Performance Bond					
Builder's Risk Insurance					
Pollution Liability					
Association Dues					
Engineering Sub					
General Conditions - Div 1					
Medium and Small Tools					
Safety					
Sales Tax					
Total Indirect Cost					
Sub-Total					
Overhead %'s		(From FMI excell calculation sheet)			
Overhead Costs					
Total Cost					
Net Profit _____ %					
Total Bid					

Fig. 2 Bid pricing sheet

Change Sheet

Once again, organization is key. Once the estimator completes his estimate and enters it onto the direct cost summary, he cannot change the entry. If he has late changes to his estimate, he enters the change to the yellow change sheet (Fig. 3). It is yellow because we don't want to lose any sheets. The sheets are numbered and recorded.

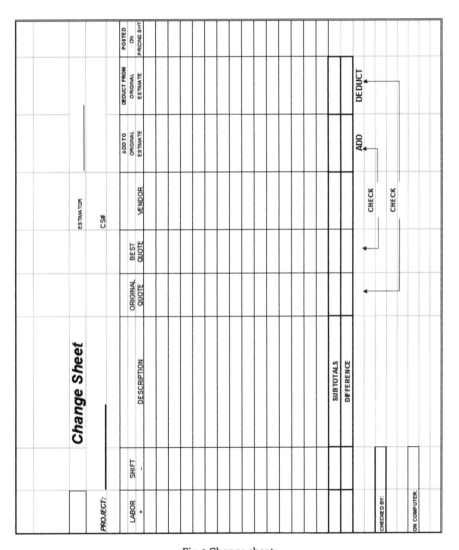

Fig. 3 Change sheet

Overhead

It was a boon to our company when we discovered and implemented dual overhead rates and variable job-size pricing created by the FMI Corporation. I don't think a lot of contractors use the FMI Overhead System. I am a firm believer in it and recommend it. It has changed our company.

Overhead is the conundrum of the construction industry. A lot of companies have gone out of business due to a lack of understanding about overhead. Overhead is what it costs to keep the doors open. Every project and every client must pay their fair share of overhead. The client does not get a discount on overhead. It is the business owner's job to know what it costs to do business, including overhead. He must know how to budget, price, and manage overhead.

The rule at Bowen is that every cost that *can* be charged to a project *should* be charged to the project. Don't put job costs in the overhead. If a senior manager or estimator is working on a specific project, his costs should go to direct job costs. The objective should be to keep as much of the cost as possible out of overhead.

I am familiar with a certain paving contractor and sometime dirt mover in Indiana. He didn't like keeping time cards for his equipment, so he charged his equipment to overhead. When he had a big equipment job, he was very competitive. When he had a job with less equipment, he was not competitive because his overhead was too high. That contractor is no longer in business. Once again, it is the business owner's responsibility to know his costs. He should know how much it costs to own and operate his construction equipment. Construction equipment is a direct job cost and must be charged directly to the job.

What is an equitable overhead rate? When I worked for Kaweah and as I started our business, I used the same overhead rate for all of our projects, regardless of size, and the same overhead rate for labor, equipment, materials, and subcontracts. It makes sense that overhead for labor should be higher than for materials and subcontractors, as labor is subject to many risks, including productivity variances, and requires supervision and management oversight. Material requires a purchase order. A larger job enjoys an economy of scale, so it makes sense that a larger job will require less overhead as a percentage.

The use of a single overhead rate always bothered me, but I didn't know how to solve it. I attended the Fails Management Institute (FMI) Pricing and Bidding Seminar in 1980. They introduced me to dual overhead rates and variable job-size pricing. The formulas and empirical charts are proprietary, but we have permission to use them. For more information about overhead management, attend the FMI Pricing and Bidding Strategy Seminar or contact FMI:

> FMI Corporation
> 5171 Glenwood Ave, Suite 200
> Raleigh, NC, 27612
> 919-787-8400
> https://www.fminet.com

The basic FMI formulas are as follows:

$$\text{Overhead rate for Materials and Subs} = \frac{\text{Overhead}}{(X) \text{ Labor} + (\text{Materials and Subs})}$$

$$\text{Overhead rate for Labor} = (X) \text{ Overhead for Materials and Subs}$$

The numbers in the formula for overhead, labor, material, and subs come from the previous year's accounting numbers. The (X) factor comes from an empirical chart provided by FMI (a portion is included in Fig. 4), and that is based on the material and sub-to-labor ratio.

The next step is to determine variable job-size pricing. We calculate the ratio between the total direct cost on a specific project and our average total direct cost from the previous year by dividing specific total direct cost by our average total direct cost (Ji/Ja). We then enter that ratio into a second empirical chart provided by FMI (a portion is included in Fig. 5) to determine the data multiplier. The data multiplier is then applied to the dual overhead rates. As an example of how the formulas work, let's calculate our overhead rates for two sample projects:

FMI Overhead Factors

(M + S)/L = Materials & Subs/Labor Ratio

(M + S)/L	X
1.0	2.46
1.1	2.53
1.2	2.59
1.3	2.66
1.4	2.72
1.5	2.79
1.6	2.86
1.7	2.93
1.8	2.99
1.9	3.06
2.0	3.13
2.1	3.19
2.2	3.26
2.3	3.33
2.4	3.39
2.5	3.46
2.6	3.53
2.7	3.59
2.8	3.66
2.9	3.72
3.0	3.79

Fig. 4 Labor X factor chart

FMI Data Multipliers for Varying Job Sizes

Ji / Ja = Ratio of individual job size to average job size

Ji / Ja	Data Multiplier
0.10	1.784
0.20	1.500
0.30	1.358
0.40	1.260
0.50	1.189
0.60	1.133
0.70	1.088
0.80	1.052
0.90	1.023
1.00	1.000
1.10	.982
1.20	.967
1.30	.956
1.40	.947
1.50	.939
1.60	.934
1.70	.930
1.80	.925
1.90	.922
2.00	.919

Fig. 5 FMI data multiplier chart

Dual Overhead Rates
1. Company financials from previous year

      a. Revenue $3,000,000

      b. Materials and Subs $1,600,000

      c. Labor (and Equipment) $800,000

      d. Total Direct Cost $2,400,000

      e. Overhead $180,000

      f. Material and Sub-to-Labor Ratio =

      $(M + S)/L = 1,600,000\ /800,000 = 2.00$

From the FMI Dual Overhead Chart (Fig. 4), $X = 3.13$

2. Dual rate for materials and subs =

Overhead / $((X)$ Labor + (Materials and Subs))

            $= 180,000\ /\ (3.13 \times 800,000 + 1,600,000)$

            $= 180,000\ /\ (2,504,000 + 1,600,000)$

            $= 180,000\ /\ 4,104,000$

            $= 4.39$ percent

3. Dual rate for labor =

(X) Overhead / (X) Labor + (Materials & Subs)

            $= 3.13 \times 180000\ /\ 4,104,000$

            $= 563,400\ /\ 4,104,000$

            $= 13.73$ percent

Variable Job Pricing
Total direct cost of the average company project $(Ja) = \$150,000$

Project A - Total Direct Cost $(Ji) = \$75,000$

      Determine overhead rates

      $Ji\ /\ Ja = 75,000\ /\ 150,000 = 0.50$

From the FMI Variable Job-Size Chart (Fig. 5) the Data Multiplier = 1.189

      Overhead rates for Project A

          $(M + S) = 1.189 \times 4.39\% = 5.22\%$

          Labor $= 1.189 \times 13.73\% = 16.32\%$

Project B - Total Direct Cost $(Ji) = \$225,000$

      Determine overhead rates

      $Ji\ /\ Ja = 225,000\ /\ 150,000 = 1.50$

      Data Multiplier = .939

      Overhead rates for Project B

          $(M + S) = 0.939 \times 4.39\% = 4.12\%$

          Labor $= 0.939 \times 13.73\% = 12.89\%$

You can see how the overhead rates change when the total direct costs go from $75,000 to $225,000. I think this formula is beautiful. We began using the FMI formulas in 1980 and I think it had a huge impact on our project pricing and financial management. In fact, we found that we were more competitive on jobs that used more material. Using the FMI system, those jobs had lower overhead rates and less risk.

In 1980, we did not have computers. We plotted our overhead rates on a semi-logarithmic graph (Fig. 6). When working on a project, we entered the total job cost and recorded the required overhead rates.

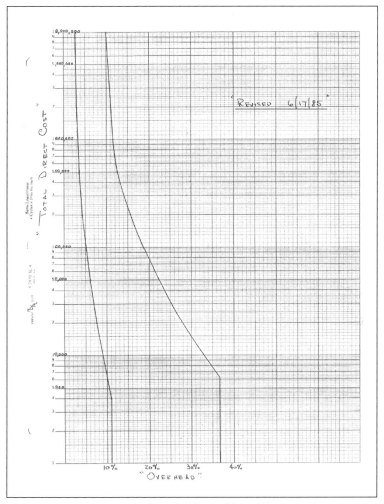

Fig. 6 FMI manual overhead - semi-logarithmic graph

Today, our overhead sheets are on a Microsoft Excel spreadsheet. We can enter the FMI formulas into the program so that overhead rates and calculations are automatic. If we get a last-minute change in our total direct cost, the program revises the overhead when the change is entered.

This computerization is extremely important when bidding public works projects, when we often get bids from subcontractors and vendors with ten minutes to go before bid closing. We believe that putting the FMI formulas on the computer has made us more competitive and helped us win jobs.

Process Equipment

In the water and wastewater business, we usually procure the engineered treatment equipment. The design engineer selects the equipment that he feels will best serve the project. That equipment is referred to as the specified "A" equipment. A contractor is often provided the opportunity to furnish "B" or equal alternate equipment, but holds the responsibility of proving that it meets the engineer's specifications.

At Bowen, we generally provide the specified "A" equipment in our bids. Providing the alternate "B" equipment creates the following potential problems:

- There is some risk associated with bidding the "B" equipment. If the engineer doesn't approve the equipment, the contractor must provide the "A" equipment at his own expense.
- The owner and his design engineer want the "A" equipment. Providing the "B" equipment is not going to generate a very good working relationship with the client.
- If the "B" equipment is provided and doesn't perform per specs, then the contractor must correct the performance at his own expense.

For managing the process equipment pricing, we use the process equipment bingo sheet (Fig. 7). The bogey number is our best guesstimate of what the equipment will cost before we have final pricing. That is the number that will go into the direct cost summary. Each column represents an equipment rep or sales agent. A rep may represent several different manufacturers on a given project. Those prices will all be listed directly under the rep's column. The final equipment price as determined on the bingo sheet will be entered onto the yellow change sheet.

Division 11 - Process Equipment Bingo Sheet

Job Name: _____

SPEC. NO.	DESCRIPTION	SPEC. MANUFACTURERS	BOGEY $	REP FIRM: NAME: PH#:	REP FIRM: NAME: PH#:	REP FIRM: NAME: PH#:	REP FIRM: NAME: PH#:	REP FIRM: NAME: PH#:
11300	Horizontal End Suction Pumps	Peerless Goulds Grundfos	$ 70,000					

Fig. 7 Process equipment bingo sheet

Bidding Strategy

The final bidding strategy must be led by an experienced manager; someone who understands the market, the competition, and the importance of optimizing the price. I define the optimum price as the low bid and 1 percent below the second place bidder.

Anyone can be a low bidder. The construction cemetery is full of low bidders. Contractors don't go out of business for lack of work. They go out of business because of cheap work.

What is your risk analysis? What can go wrong on a project and how do you evaluate it? Where is your greatest exposure? At Bowen Engineering, we have identified labor as our biggest risk and value it at 40 percent of the labor budget. A contractor can only cover that risk with profit and contingency. Unfortunately, profit and contingency seldom cover our risk. So it is imperative that we recognize the risk and manage well.

Contingency

Every bid and potential project has a certain level of unknowns. Sometimes we recognize the unknowns, but sometimes we don't know what we don't know. You may have unclear specifications, drawings that are incomplete, complex work activities that you don't fully understand, and there may be bid mistakes. You may have difficult operations that raise the risk. Just by their level of difficulty, you know that things are going to go wrong.

The savvy bid manager has to recognize the level of uncertainty. He allows for that uncertainty by adding a contingency. In the private market and on design-build projects, contingency is standard practice. But a contingency should also be added to public works projects. There are still unknowns. Every bid should have some level of contingency.

Owner Furnished Equipment

At Bowen Engineering we occasionally run into a project where the owner provides the process equipment. They purchase the equipment to eliminate contractor markup on the pricing and purchase of the equipment. The contractor is still required to install the equipment, do the necessary startup, and whatever other activities are associated with the equipment.

Nothing in the project changes for the contractor. The risk, complexity and activities are the same, but the contractor is expected to reduce his overall markup. You can argue that the owner is required to expedite delivery. But the savvy contractor needs to stay involved in scheduling delivery because it will impact the master schedule. The problem with the owner expediting delivery is that he has no skin in the game.

At Bowen we use the FMI variable job size pricing. If the owner provides the process equipment the overhead rates will automatically increase.

If you accept our premise that risk equals forty percent of labor, and you remove furnishing process equipment from the contractor's work package, risk as a percentage of total contract cost goes up. The savvy bid manager will reflect this in his pricing strategy. You should not bid the same profit that you would on a standard labor and materials contract. The contractor deserves a fair profit.

Bidding strategy requires leadership, savvy, and a little courage. Anyone can be low bidder. When he was president of Bowen, Jed Holt studied all of the bids we had won over a two- year period. If we had raised all of our bids by 1 percent, we would not have lost any of those bids.

Lessons Learned

- Use dual overhead rates.
- Use variable job-size overhead pricing.
- Every project must pay its fair share of overhead.
- Expenses should be charged to direct job cost whenever possible.
- Optimize your bid pricing. Anyone can be low bidder.

5

FINANCIAL MANAGEMENT

"Cash is king."
– Fred S. Klipsch, retired chairman,
Klipsch Audio Technologies

I worked up a financial history of our first ten years in business (Fig. 1). I included a ten year financial history for a reason. When Bowen Engineering does strategic planning and one year business planning, we use a ten year financial history as shown in figure 1. When I attended Harvard most of our case studies included a ten year financial history. It shows what has happened in the past and helps the planners project future business. I also think it is kind of interesting on how we progressed in those first ten years.

We grew contract revenues at a rate of almost 50 percent per year. You can do that with a startup. It is hard to do with a mature company. We averaged 11.2 percent gross margin and 5.4 percent net return on sales. Our net return on equity after taxes was 28.4 percent, compared to our initial goal of 20 percent. We were profitable every year except the first year, and our equity grew by nine times. These numbers are good. Are they great? Possibly not. We are certainly not an IBM or a Microsoft. But we never intended to be. Our goals were to start a sound company, do things the right way, build an organization, and make a reasonable return on investment. The important thing is that we paid our bills, we were

BOWEN ENGINEERING
TEN YEAR FINANCIAL HISTORY

	1968	1969	1970	1971	1972	1973	1974	1975	1976	1977	AVERAGE
Income Statement											
Revenue	165,000	265,569	599,712	553,789	1,212,709	2,195,320	2,174,379	2,924,483	2,134,027	3,397,244	
Growth %		61.0%	125.8%	-7.7%	119.0%	81.0%	-1.0%	34.5%	-27.0%	59.2%	49.4%
Direct Costs (COG)	161,299	237,948	512,930	473,210	1,058,448	1,928,375	1,964,773	2,663,418	1,981,578	3,167,434	
Gross Profit	3,701	27,621	86,782	80,579	154,261	266,945	209,606	261,065	152,449	229,810	
Gross Profit (%/rev)	2.3%	11.6%	16.9%	17.0%	14.6%	13.8%	10.7%	9.8%	7.7%	7.3%	11.2%
Overhead	8,065	11,897	25,647	23,661	52,922	96,419	98,239	133,171	99,079	158,372	
Total Cost	169,364	249,845	538,577	496,871	1,111,370	2,024,794	2,063,012	2,796,589	2,080,657	3,325,806	
Net Job Profit	-4,364	15,724	61,135	56,918	101,339	170,526	111,367	127,894	53,370	71,438	
Net Job Profit (%/rev)	-2.6%	5.9%	10.2%	10.3%	8.4%	7.8%	5.1%	4.4%	2.5%	2.1%	5.4%
Dividends, Taxes, Adjust	0	0	13,099	40,396	-19,635	122,704	-7,107	202,672	74,376	16,426	
Profit After Div, Tax, Adjust	-4,364	15,724	48,036	16,522	120,974	47,822	118,474	-74,778	-21,006	55,012	
Financial Analysis											
Net Return on Equity	-9.7%	38.7%	85.2%	15.8%	100.0%	19.8%	40.9%	-18.3%	-6.3%	17.5%	28.4%
Equity ($45,000)	40,636	56,360	104,396	120,918	241,892	289,714	408,188	333,410	312,404	367,416	
Comments							Changed to Sub-S				

Fig. 1 Ten Year Financial History

profitable and we were still in business. The bank and the bonding company loved us.

My policy was never to surprise the bank or the bonding company. Accordingly, in 1976 we got off to a terrible start. At the end of six months, we were $50,000 in the hole. I asked our bank and bonding company to attend a meeting at my office, to review our first six months and our future projections. I explained what had happened in our operations and why we were in the red. I presented a detailed analysis of how we would recover our initial losses and show a profit by the end of the fiscal year. We made $53,000 that year (Fig. 1). I think the only job that made a profit that year was the DeMotte Sewage Treatment Plant, which was run by Gary Moon. He was onsite full time as superintendent and project manager.

Equity Requirements

How much equity do you need to run a business? If you are a regular general contractor doing public works or local construction, equity should be 10 percent of annual revenue. That is a conservative number. We ran into trouble at Tennessee Valley Authority (TVA) in 2009, and our equity at the time was 10 percent of annual revenue. Our cash reserves kept us going very nicely (see chapter thirteen).

Today, we are in the industrial power market. Some owners are asking for irrevocable letters of credit (LOC) in lieu of performance bonds. Why an owner would want a 10 or 20 percent LOC in lieu of a 100 percent performance bond makes no sense. The cost impact to the owner is about the same. The cost impact to the contractor is not the same. The bank treats LOC's like loans. LOC's are charged against the company's credit line.

Work in the industrial power market is also more complicated and risky. The jobs are larger and farther from home. I think the equity-to-revenue ratio should be a minimum of 20 percent. Cash is king. You don't want to run out of cash when facing problems. I think the big companies carry 25 percent equity to revenue.

Year-End Bonus Plan

For every dollar that Bowen makes in net income, twenty-five cents goes to our employees in the form of an end-of-year bonus. This is in addition to our retirement plan contributions. We got the idea from one of our board members. Our employees work hard. They should be able to share in the company profits that they helped create. I want them to love working at Bowen Engineering, and I love getting those thank-yous.

I asked one of my engineering friends how much they put aside for employee bonuses. He said 15 percent. I don't know what other companies do for their bonuses, but my sense is that we are pretty unique.

Billings/Cash Flow

Construction is unlike any other industry. You typically work for a month, bill the owner at the end of the period, and hopefully receive payment thirty days later, if the owner pays you on time. Figure it out; some of the work performed at the beginning of the period is sixty days old.

If that isn't bad enough, the owner often withholds 10 percent retention until the end of the project, as protection against the contractor's performance. Construction is the only industry that does this. If you buy a watch or a car, you pay for it before you leave the store. Today's contractor is expected to provide short-term financing for the project. A contractor must be aware of the payment terms and take appropriate action wherever possible, as follows:

- Submit all month-end invoices on time. You would be surprised at the number of contractors who are too busy to send in their monthly invoices.
- Front-end load your overhead and supervisory costs. Most of your overhead and supervisory costs are spent on the early part of the project. These costs should be billed when they are spent.
- Pay subcontractors and major vendors when you get paid. "Pay when paid." Typically, you pay a sub/vendor ten days after receipt of payment from the owner. It is written into the subcontract or purchase order. Giving them better terms is being gapped.

- Negotiate 5 percent retention. You don't have to accept 10 percent, unless it is a government job.
- Insist on net 15 payment terms. You don't have to accept net 30, unless it is a government job.

Dr. Emol A. Fails, PhD, founder of Fails Management Institute (now FMI Corporation) says, "If a contractor doesn't have time to send his invoices out, he doesn't have time to be in business." This is called managing cash flow. Cash is king. A contractor should not be expected to finance the project for anything other than contractual retentions and normal payment cycles.

I had a friend who sold bird seed to a major supply house. The payment terms were net 90. It put him out of business. Then there was the subcontractor who had received payment for materials stored. Instead of paying the material supplier, he purchased a new Cadillac. He said we could not tell him how he must spend his money. Wrong. We are trustees for our subcontractor and vendor money. We must be good stewards. It is not our money.

Improving Margin

We had our only year-end loss in 2011, other than our first year. We had several jobs that came in substantially over our costs. We had a basic problem in that we would generally project a net profit through the course of the job, only to lose money at the end. This was happening consistently on much of our work.

Our CEO, Doug Bowen, implemented a system to correct the situation and hopefully prevent the situation from happening again. First of all, he and senior management began holding 30, 50 and 70 percent reviews of each major project onsite with the management team. They examine what has happened on the project to date and what can we expect of the project when it is finished. This is still early enough to course correct.

At the 30 percent point, we know enough about what to expect on the project. At the 70 percent point, it is still not too late to effect any needed cures. We should know what is waiting for us and what we need to be aware of to close out the project.

Doug's next change was to begin holding quarterly reviews with senior management and the individual management teams on each project. They look at four statistics:

1. Contract profit to date
2. Expected contract profit at completion
3. Opportunities to improve margin
4. Possible dangers that may create profit fade

This approach has created a major change in the cost management of all of our projects. Bowen developed a Job Cost Profit-and-Loss Report (Fig. 2) that is now used in our company cost management and is presented to the board of directors at each board meeting.

Our president and CEO is focused on project costs. He spends his time and effort to analyze each project on a regular basis. As a result, the entire company is also focused and our cost management is better than ever. You cannot manage what you don't measure.

Equipment Costing

Bowen owns its own construction equipment. We believe that we can provide our own equipment for less than we can rent. We don't have a markup and there is a repetitive usage component that further reduces the cost.

A lot of contractors rent their equipment. They keep their cash. We don't operate that way. I like owning our equipment, I think it makes us a contractor. The good news is that our CEO, Doug Bowen, agrees with me.

We don't make a profit on our equipment. We charge our equipment to our projects at cost. Our number one objective is Bowen Engineering. How do we make the mother ship more competitive and thereby more successful? We believe that having our equipment as a profit center would be counter-productive. Some construction companies keep the construction equipment as a separate company. This then becomes a source of additional income for the owners.

We provide the highest quality construction equipment. When it gets tired, we don't spend a small fortune rebuilding it, we trade it in and get a newer model. When our customers see us roll onto a new job, they see relatively new, state-of-the-art construction equipment. I think it enhances our image.

PROJECT	CONTRACT AMOUNT	% COMPLETE	BENCHMARK PROFIT	EST'D NET PROFIT AT COMPL	NET PROFIT TO DATE	CHANGES TO DATE	POTENTIAL GAIN	POTENTIAL FADE

QUARTERLY JOB COST PROFIT AND LOSS REPORT

PERIOD ENDING:

POTENTIAL CHANGES

Fig. 2 Quarterly profit and loss report

A contractor has to know what it costs him to own and operate construction equipment. Our cost analysis includes insurance, depreciation, maintenance, fuel costs, and interest if there is an outstanding equipment loan. Equipment manufacturers contend that we should figure in replacement cost. I think that is covered by depreciation. I may lose that argument. Once again, how do we make the mother ship more competitive?

I studied accounting at Purdue University. It has helped us as we started our business. It is important to have good accounting principles in the business. You have to know what it costs to do business.

Lessons Learned

- Senior management needs to review the project costs on a regular basis.
- Negotiate 5 percent retention. You don't have to accept 10 percent.
- Negotiate net 15 payment terms. You don't have to accept net 30.
- Equity should be at least 10 percent of annual revenue.
- A generous bonus pool works.
- Ask, "How do we improve margin?"
- Subcontractors are "pay when paid."

6

MANAGEMENT TEAMS

"The main ingredient of stardom is the rest of the team."
– John Wooden, Purdue legend and basketball All-American

Construction is a competitive sport. At Bowen Engineering, our goal is to be the champion. We are trying to be winners and beat the competition. It is like a good football team. Each player must do his job and we all must work together.

In 1975, we were struggling. Our project managers were overloaded. They were managing their projects and in addition, they were bidding new work. They didn't have enough time to manage anything effectively. Since the bids had deadlines, estimating got the attention and managing the projects under contract suffered. Tom Greve, senior manager at Bowen, came up with the idea of establishing management teams.

We assigned a management staff to each project manager. This enabled the project manager to delegate much of the work and manage the estimating and construction more effectively. The typical staff included the following:

- Project manager
- Project engineer
- Superintendent
- Foremen (we self-perform 75 percent of the project)
- Project coordinator

We may have several project engineers and superintendents on a larger project. Today, our entire operations are made up of management teams. Every project manager has a project engineer, a superintendent, and a project coordinator. Look at the organization chart for the Duke Gibson Water Redirect Project (Fig. 1). The project manager is Pat Meunier and the project superintendent is John Eastes. Eastes has six area superintendents and there are four project engineers serving as assistant superintendents. They report to the area superintendents. This is typical for a large power project.

The job of a project manager is very complicated. He has lots of problems to solve, lots of people to manage, and he fills the role of several different functions. Those functions can best be described as follows:

- Chief executive officer
- Chief financial officer
- Contract administrator
- Marketing director/public relations
- Historian

In reality, he is running his own business entity. These responsibilities are daunting if you stop to think about them in total. And he has to get others to do his bidding, bring the project in on budget, and satisfy a client.

The management teams concept was a total success. Our company has developed a management team culture that has brought us planning, leadership, and zero injuries. To further ease the bottleneck, we have also added central estimating, and they do most of the takeoff and pricing. The project manager is involved in the bidding and helps make the final decision on pricing.

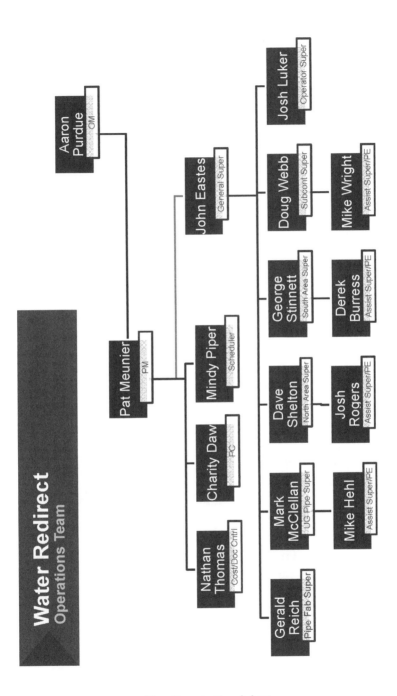

Fig. 1 Organizational chart

Hiring the Best

I started with the W. M. Lyles Company in 1962. They had been hiring recent college graduates for at least ten years before I joined the company. In doing so, they were way ahead of their time. Mr. W. M. Lyles himself, the founder of the W.M. Lyles Company and a Purdue grad, hired me. I thought this practice was a great idea, so when I started my own company, I hired new college grads. We interviewed at Purdue University and Rose Hulman University as early as 1970. In order for Bowen to be a well-run professional organization, I knew that I had to interview at the universities and staff our company with college graduates, just like the big companies. Our customers like dealing with engineering professionals. We hired Gary Moon out of Rose Hulman University in 1973. He was one of our first hires. Moon recently completed forty years of service at Bowen and is still going strong.

Today, Bowen has more graduate engineers per dollar of volume than any contractor in the United States. We boast one graduate engineer per every $3 million of volume. It amazes me that so many smaller companies are unwilling to hire more young college graduates. We also hire college interns. In 2016, we employed forty interns from universities around the Midwest.

What do the great football coaches like Vince Lombardi, Tom Landry, Don Shula, and Bill Walsh have in common? They have great players. It is also true for great construction companies. They have great players. In order to be successful in construction, you must have talented people.

We were always on the lookout for great employees. Our second major project was the Jamestown Sewage Treatment Plant. Hurst Excavating was installing the sewers in Jamestown. Their superintendent and heavy equipment operator was Bob Newman. Newman did some excavating work for us on our project. About three years later (1973), he called and said he was leaving Hurst and was looking for a job. I hired him on the spot, even though I didn't have any work for him. I knew a good man when I saw him and I had no trouble putting him to work. Newman got us into the sewer business, which we still handle today. We couldn't possibly have gone into the sewer business without him. Newman retired from Bowen Engineering in 2005.

One of our other great hires was Tom Greve. He was a salesman for Pollution Control Inc., who manufactured package sewage treatment plants. We were a fairly good customer of Pollution Control. Greve's style was high energy and he was a very good salesman. He had a positive attitude, excellent values, and leadership skills. I thought Greve would help us build a better company. He was a little reluctant to hire on, so I recruited his wife to help us convince him. Greve hired on as a project manager in 1978 and retired in 2009. He also hired good people. He hired many of our senior leaders who have had a tremendous impact on the success of our company.

The Importance of Support Staff

The Holy Grail of the management teams concept is the project coordinator (PC). Many smaller companies today do not provide coordinators or assistants for their project managers. Adopting this important role was the decision that changed our company. Our first PC was Terry Boho. She was our receptionist at the time. She was over qualified for the receptionist job and she only took it because our office was close to her home. She had business talent, was very outgoing, and very savvy. She was a natural to become our first PC. Our second PC was Cindy Gilbertson, who today runs her own company. We had two very talented people to begin the process and it contributed greatly to our success. Today, we have twelve project coordinators in the company. We are recognized for our project coordinators.

The project coordinator is more than an administrative assistant. This is a person who has construction experience, college education, and often a college degree. The coordinator has responsibility for several areas in the construction process, including invoicing, submittal logs, delivery and work schedules for subs and vendors, and coordination of team activities.

Managing invoicing is a critical area. In the early days, we struggled to get our invoices out on time. We learned quickly that if you don't have time to get your invoices out, you don't get paid. No one gets their invoices out any better than Bowen Engineering, thanks to our project coordinators.

With a project coordinator on the team, there is always someone there to take the customer's call. And it is someone they know. The customer doesn't get a computer, a receptionist, or a voice mail box. And that someone can get moving on whatever the issue is.

The project coordinator gives the project manager the opportunity and time to do his job. The project manager doesn't get mired down in mundane activities that can be done by a more junior member of the team. The good news is that we have a player on the team that adds value. Our clients and associates love our project coordinators.

We hold training sessions for our project managers, project engineers, superintendents, and project coordinators, within their groups, twice each year. In addition, the project managers and superintendents have a joint training session annually. The objective is training, but the greater benefit is developing family and sharing experiences and values.

A leader must build an organization. At Bowen, we have built our company by creating management teams, recruiting young college graduates, and hiring outstanding leaders from the construction industry. We want our project managers to manage people, not concrete. The project manager must delegate to his staff. He must have time to think. He can only do that if he has a management team. He then must nurture his staff so that they can develop their management skills.

It is amazing to see the number of smaller construction companies that don't provide their project managers with support staff. They are afraid to make the investment. Do the math. Many of the duties of the project management can be done by a project coordinator at half the cost. The same goes for a project engineer. A project manager can run more projects, more effectively, if he has a good support team.

To be successful today, you must be organized, hire good people, and bring people together. Moon said it best: "We want to keep our small company values."

Lessons Learned

- Establish the role of project coordinator.
- Create management teams.
- Supervision is not expensive. Staff your company.
- Always be on the lookout for talented people.
- Conduct ongoing, in-house management training.

7

LEADERSHIP

"The task of a leader is to get his/her people from where they are to where they have never been."
– Henry Kissinger

Leadership is a culture. It is everyone's business and is ongoing. Leaders are not born, they are developed. We are all looking for leadership.

In 1997, we completed $50 million in volume. We had been in business thirty years and had eight to ten leaders. By 2008, we were at $360 million in volume and had fifty leaders. We had grown $300 million in eleven years. You can't survive unless you grow. You can't grow unless you develop deep leadership skills within your team. No one can do it alone.

At Bowen, we conduct leadership training for our project managers, project engineers, and superintendents. We use a program entitled "The Leadership Challenge®," based on *The Leadership Challenge: How to Make Extraordinary Things Happen in Organizations* by James Kouzes and Barry Posner (San Francisco: Jossey-Bass, 2007). Kouzes and Posner have been providing leadership training materials since 1980 and are considered by most people in the industry to be the best.

If you are interested in expanding your leadership training, you can contact the distributor for Kouzes and Posner. They also provide instructor training. I attended their training course, The Leadership Challenge® Workshop before we launched our leadership training program at Bowen Engineering.

International Leadership Associates
2 Sheila Court
Hamilton, OH, 45013
Steve Coats
stevec@i-lead.com
(513) 755-7112

In *The Leadership Challenge,* Kouzes and Posner define leadership as "the art of mobilizing others to want to struggle for shared aspirations." It is an art. And it takes a team. If it were easy, everyone would do it. Hopefully, we are all headed in the same direction.

Let's examine the difference between management and leadership. Below you will find listed the primary tasks of a manager and a leader:

Management	Leadership
Planning	Setting direction
Organizing	Aligning
Staffing	Inspiring
Controlling	Setting vision
Problem solving	Making a difference

Let's look at these differences in a broader sense:

Management	Leadership
Promoting stability	Promoting change
Dealing with process	Dealing with people

It isn't just about concrete and pipe, it's about people. We need managers and we need leaders. Not everyone is good at both. At Bowen, our top managers are good at both. We are trying to drive accountability and responsibility to the lowest level of management.

Many older managers and most young managers tend to be micro-managers. They do everything themselves. They are usually college graduates and they feel that no one can do their job as well as they can, when in fact, if they are to really be successful, they must teach and train others to do their jobs and to grow. Bowen board member,

Dave Pedersen, of Sage Inc. says, "Leaders are measured by their followers."

My step son, Chris Stater, was promoted to project manager at the computer software company where he worked. He asked me for advice on how to be successful. I said, "Focus on your staff. Make them successful. If they are successful, you will be successful." It is not about you. Let's look at some of the best ways to contribute to employee success.

FIVE PRACTICES OF EXEMPLARY LEADERSHIP®

Kouzes and Posner have broken their program into the Five Practices of Exemplary Leadership®. I have listed Kouzes' and Posner's five practices below, but I have modified a few of the titles, shown in parentheses.

- Model the Way (Personal Values)
- Inspire a Shared Vision
- Enable Others to Act (Communications)
- Challenge the Process (Change Management)
- Encourage the Heart

We developed a management training program for our young managers and superintendents. It is made up of seven sessions, including an introduction, sessions on each of the five leadership practices, and a final celebration session. The final session is at a resort-type locale and spouses also attend. The details of the program are as follows:

- Each participant is assigned to a senior management mentor. Each participant is provided access to an outside professional coach.
- The training sessions are held every two months.
- Each session is four hours in length.
- Sessions are taught by Bowen senior management.
- A dinner is held the night before each session and an outside industry leader is brought in to kick it off.
- Each student is required to complete a community service project during the year, and present on it at the final celebration session.

As part of the training program, the students participate in the Leadership Practices Inventory® (LPI), developed by Kouzes and Posner. They complete a survey that identifies their leadership strengths and weaknesses. The survey is also completed by five outside observers, who may be fellow workers, or bosses. The results compare the student's perception of his leadership skills against the perception of those around him.

The inventory looks at thirty leadership behaviors. The student can look at the lowest scoring behaviors to determine where he should focus his effort to improve his leadership skills. If the student scores himself higher than his observers for specific behaviors, then this might indicate that his opinion of himself is different from others' perceptions. Their perception is his reality. The inventory is designed to measure specific leadership behaviors and will contribute towards his development as a leader.

Also, as part of the program, the students are asked to report on their personal best leadership experience. The student is asked to relate an experience in his life when he was in a leadership position or situation. He is asked to answer:

- Who – was involved?
- What – challenges did you face?
- Where – did it take place?
- When – did it happen?
- How – did you respond to the challenge?
- Lessons learned?

Model the Way – Personal Values

I attended an expanded executive training program at Harvard called Owner President Management (OPM). As we talked about leadership, my professor suggested that the two most important characteristics of a leader are:

- High values and standards
- Demonstrating genuine concern for others

When I worked at Lyles, Bill Brown told me that success in construction is based on two things:

- Paying attention to detail
- Demonstrating genuine concern for others

Leadership is a dialogue. A leader must focus on others. Do you follow through? Do you do what you say you will do? When you are promoted, whether it be to a new position or a new project, the questions you will be asked are:

- Who are you?
- What are your values?
- What is your vision?
- Do you care about me?
- Are you extraordinary?

One of our carpenter superintendents once told me, "They don't care how much you know until they know how much you care." Workers/employees won't believe the message unless they believe the messenger.

Why do people quit a job? Consensus in the industry is that 70 percent of the time, people quit a company because of their direct supervisor, not because of the company. They don't leave for better money or a better opportunity; they leave because they can't work for their boss.

How do you evaluate a company? Look at its people. Are they proud and do they love working there? What impact do they have on the community? Are they engaged in the community? Giving back is an essential part of leadership.

For my part, I want my young employees to think like a contractor. I want them to be tough. If they are not going to be tough, then they shouldn't be in the construction business.

We are looking for "get with-it" guys/gals. We are looking for people who make things happen, take responsibility, and are tough minded. We want them to:

- Be competitive
- Have high expectations
- Never give up
- Have some urgency
- Make lemonade out of lemons
- Challenge the process
- Over-communicate
- Sell themselves

Inspire a Shared Vision

When you are planning and getting ready to start that next project, what is your vision? What do you tell your team? What are the goals of the project? What do you want people to say about your team at the end?

I tell my young project managers and my students that they can use the following questions as a checklist for success. If they achieve these goals, they will be successful. So many of our project managers are just there to build the job. No! You are there to improve the process, to raise the bar.

Project Vision
- Did we send everyone home safe?
- Did we improve margin?
- Did we develop staff?
- Did we delight the client?
- Did we finish the job early?
- Did we improve communications?
- Did we have fun?

How about delighting the client? Thirty years ago, I told my employees that if you don't delight the client, you don't deserve to make a profit. They laughed at me. But it is true. We provide a service to our clients. That service includes quality, cooperation, communication, and teamwork. If we don't deliver the goods, we shouldn't be in business.

When I was a youngster, they said, "Seeing is believing." They have it backwards. You have to believe that you can be a leader and that you can make a difference. You have to believe that you can develop staff and a team. You have to believe that you can delight the client. You have to believe that you can have zero injuries. Only then will you see it.

My first big project was in 1964. It was the Ojai Sewage Treatment Plant, just north of Los Angeles. I had bid the job and now I was the on-site project manager. My family and I moved from the San Joaquin Valley to Los Angeles. This was the first time a project manager had moved from the home office to live on site for a Kaweah project.

My vision was that this would be the greatest job of all time and that I would be recognized as the greatest project manager of all time. It was a reasonably successful job. We made a modest profit and finished the job on time. I didn't get much recognition, but I had a vision.

Anyone can steer the boat, but it takes a leader to chart the course. What is your vision?

Enable Others to Act – Communications

We all think of ourselves as good communicators. We are not. This misconception is exacerbated by the fact that most construction people are hard-wired, left-brain engineers and technicians. They deal with formulas and metrics. As leaders, we need to expand our right brains, or soft skills, which include empathy and genuine concern for others.

How do we communicate? Albert Mehrabian, professor emeritus of psychology, UCLA, developed what has become known as the 7%-38%-55% Rule, for the relative impact of words, tone of voice, and body language when speaking (Mehrabian, A. and Wiener, M., 1967, "Decoding of Inconsistent Communications", *Journal of Personality and Social Psychology*, 6, 109-114 and Mehrabian, A., and Ferris, S.R., 1967, "Inference of Attitudes from Nonverbal Communication in Two Channels", *Journal of Consulting Psychology*, 31, 3, 48-258). His studies show three elements in any face-to-face communication:

- Verbal (spoken words) – 7 percent
- Action (voice and tone) – 38 percent
- Attitude (body language) – 55 percent

The non-verbal elements convey the speaker's inner thoughts and feelings and may contradict the speaker's words. We think that we communicate verbally, but in fact, we communicate most often through our actions and attitudes. You can determine the success or failure of a subordinate simply by your attitude. If you believe in the person, they will have a good chance of success. If you don't believe in the person, they will have little chance of success.

I had a chief financial officer (CFO) with whom I was only marginally happy. Instead of helping him solve his problems, I made it pretty clear that I did not believe in him. He had little chance of success, if for no other reason than my attitude. He finally left the company under very stressful conditions. I regret my behavior. As

I go forward, I try to use that experience in my dealings with my subordinates.

How important is listening? Great leaders listen 80 percent of the time. You cannot speak and listen at the same time. I use a tool called "Three Ear Listening," which I learned from the American Management Association, by asking three important questions:

1. What are they saying?
2. What are they "not" saying?
3. What do they want to say, but don't because of fear?

A leader must understand his audience, know his self-worth, and learn to keep his mouth shut.

How important is feedback? How do you know how you are doing? I have been criticized by my subordinates for not getting feedback on my own performance. That is the beauty of the LPI Survey, which is part of our in-house leadership training program. You have to ask your fellow workers, "How am I doing?" Bowen's past president, Jed Holt, did a 360-degree survey with his direct reports. He wasn't really happy with the results, but he did it. In our company, that took a lot of courage.

Good communicators practice six key principles:

- Over-communicate – keep the team informed
- Formal communications – you can't communicate by accident
- One-on-one coaching – meet regularly with subordinates
- Sell your ideas – build consensus
- Use the "we" word – it is not "your" job, it is "our" job
- There is no winner and loser - everyone wins with good communications

You are the leader. You are the boss. Good communications are your responsibility. It is critical that the leader take responsibility for communications.

Challenge the Process – Change Management

In *The Leadership Challenge*, (San Francisco: Jossey-Bass, 2008, 184), Kouzes and Posner say that "The focus of a leader's attention should be less on the routine operations and much more on the untested and untried. Leaders should always be asking what's new? What's next? What's better? That's where the future is."

The industry is constantly changing. If we always do what we've always done, we'll always get what we've always gotten. If a contractor is going to survive, he must change and grow. Take our competitors in 1967, for example. They are all gone. Look at American businesses such as Xerox, Polaroid, and the railroad industry. They all failed to change with the times. At Bowen, we recognize our need to stay current. Here are some of the initiatives that we have implemented:

- Management teams
- Preplanning culture – started in 1980
- New markets:
  - Sewer business – Bob Newman helped us launch this business in 1980.
  - Micro tunneling in 1990 – It didn't work and we are out of that business.
  - Structural steel erection – Started in 2004. It got us into the power industry.
- Lean construction – from the Toyota Way – started in 2000
- Marketing culture – now doing 90 percent private work
- Performance contracting – design-build in the public works arena
- Zero injury culture

Challenge is the opportunity for greatness. Leaders look for innovative ways to improve their work and their organization. Innovation comes from listening. Leaders seek out good ideas and challenge the system for implementation. Albert Einstein said it best: "Imagination is more important than knowledge." Leaders step into the unknown.

Great leaders are learners. They take risks, and that involves mistakes and failures. You have to experiment and take risks to find better ways of doing things. There is no better teacher than failure. We learn more from our mistakes than from any other learning format. NFL coaches Tom Landry, Chuck Noll, Bill Walsh, and Jimmy Johnson in their first seasons were a collective four wins, fifty-three losses, and one tie. Between them, they have won thirteen Super Bowls. Someone believed in them and gave them the freedom to fail.

Great leaders are also great problem solvers. They achieve success by creating small wins. Small wins create a pattern of winning. Leaders break big problems into small manageable pieces. They find ways to make it easy to succeed. To generate small wins:

- Break it down
- Keep it simple
- Do the easy part first
- Accumulate yeses
- Give feedback
- Celebrate

Encourage the Heart

Encouraging the heart is the final piece of the puzzle. When I started my company, I knew one thing; I wanted my employees to love working at Bowen Engineering. We do everything possible to be sure they share in the company's success. Here are some of our best practices:

- Twenty-five cents of every dollar of company profit goes to the employees in the form of profit sharing.
- Our top employees are stockholders and own half of Bowen Engineering.
- Every employee has an opportunity to do an outstanding job.
- Training is provided for every employee.
- Esprit de corps is a standard at Bowen Engineering.
- Employees have a voice in how business is done.
- CEO Doug Bowen holds a town hall meeting every quarter.

In 2007, Bowen was ranked by the Great Place to Work Institute and the Society of Human Resource Management as the nineteenth best place to work in America for medium-sized companies. In 2008, we were ninth. The ranking is determined by survey of a company's employees. Our employees are engaged.

You have to build up your people by recognizing their work and celebrating their success. They enjoy being recognized and they love to celebrate. How do you do that? You engage with employees' families at company events. You provide safety lunches on the jobsite. You create excitement. You spend time with the troops and the team.

All of your employees want to be on a winning team. Construction is a team sport. You win when everyone is playing well. Many young managers think they have a lock on wanting to win. All of our employees have their favorite NFL football team. They can feel the same excitement about their employer. It is up to the leader to help create that excitement.

I tell our project managers, and my students at Purdue, if they want to be successful, they must develop their leadership skills. It takes more than concrete.

Lessons Learned

- The bottom line is that we are looking for leadership. Leadership impacts every facet of a business. You cannot survive unless you grow. You cannot grow without leadership.
- Leadership not only impacts the business, but it also impacts your personal life. Your family is looking for leadership. If you are a student, your university and your professors are looking for leadership.
- You have to believe you can lead. Only then will you see it.
- To be a great leader, you must be imaginative.
- You must have good personal values.
- You must genuinely care about others.

8

POSITIVE ATTITUDE AND SOCIAL INTELLIGENCE

*"College graduates will be hired for their technical skills.
They will be promoted for their personal skills."*
– Russell Clough, professor, Stanford University

I have always been a reasonably positive guy. But as I have grown older, I have expanded my positive attitude. I believe in my heart that as I have become more positive, I have been more effective and successful as a leader. The leader's persona permeates the entire company. Our company has developed a very strong esprit de corps. I have been told on several occasions that when you walk into our office, you see that esprit de corps in the foyer. This spirit has had an impact on our company's success and I take some credit for that.

In *Power vs Force: An Anatomy of Consciousness* (New York: Hay House Inc., 2012, 95-121), David M. Hawkins, MD, PhD, has analyzed the levels of human consciousness. In it, he examines the energy level of different attitudes and emotions. I was introduced to Hawkins' material by Dan Suwyn, partner, Workplace Dynamics. Suwyn has presented Hawkins' material in the form of the Courage Scale (Fig. 1).

Hawkins has determined energy levels for all of humanity. The dividing line is courage. If a person falls below the courage line, he sees life as hopeless and frightening, but above the courage line, life is seen as exciting, challenging and stimulating. The scale is logarithmic. So, 300 is not twice as great as 150; it is 300 to the tenth power greater than 150 to the tenth power. As we move up the scale, the increase in energy is enormous.

Hawkins says that 85 percent of the world's population is below the courage line and these individuals are energy takers. Fifteen percent of the world's population is above the courage line and these individuals are energy givers. The average is 204.

The Courage Scale

By David R. Hawkins, M.D.

Level	Log	
Enlightenment	700 – 1000	
Peace	600	
Joy	540	
Love	500	
Reason/Logic	400	
Willingness	310	
Openness	250	GIVING
Courage	200	
Anger	150	TAKING
Fear	100	
Grief	75	
Apathy	50	
Guilt	30	
Shame	20	
Death	0	

Fig. 1 Courage scale

It takes courage to be an energy giver. Energy givers are constructive, positive, and are directed towards vitality and vibrancy. Energy takers drain energy from those around them and those individuals' energy spirals downward. Go back to chapter seven and examine the fifth exemplary practice, "Encourage the Heart." By breaking down the word "encourage," you get the word "courage," which is an essential part of encouragement.

Fred Klipsch, retired chairman, Klipsch Audio Technologies, has started and run several successful businesses. He says, "I don't want any negative from my employees." A good leader must be an energy giver. He must present a positive attitude. And he must develop a positive attitude in his team. If he is positive, his team will be positive. Conversely, if he is negative, his team will be negative. A leader cannot bring his personal disappointments and emotions to the office. Everyone on his team is watching. If he is down, everyone will be down.

Hawkins has identified several individuals and roles; on the courage scale:

- Skilled tradesmen   High 200's
- Project managers   300
- Senior managers   350
- Company executives   400
- Einstein   500
- Freud   500
- Who ?   1,000

Suwyn has developed a four-step action plan when using the courage scale:

1. Recognize when we personally fall "below the line."
2. Gain skills to bring ourselves back up "above the line."
3. Gains skills that invite others to move "above the line."
4. Create work environments that live "above the line."

Doug Bowen, Bowen Engineering's CEO, says it best: "Attitude equals altitude." He loves the message from the US Navy's Blue Angels: the more positive you are, the higher you will soar.

How do you become enthusiastic? By having a passion for your job? By being successful? By having more fun? By reading a book? Drinking an elixir? Seeing a shrink? Maybe a better question is, how do you develop your social circuitry?

There is only one way! Undertake the hard work of changing your behavior. Develop a personal vision for change. You can start by doing a diagnostic assessment by completing the LPI Survey in Kouzes and Posner's Leadership Challenge (see chapter seven).

The more enthusiastic you are, the better leader you will be. That is not to say that you will not be a good leader if you are a dullard. But you will be a better leader if you have a positive attitude. Great leaders elicit laughter from their subordinates three times as often as average leaders. Laughter is serious business.

Social Intelligence

I think that developing leader-managers is complicated because many of our young managers tend to be micro managers. The goal of leadership development is further complicated by the fact that they are mostly engineers and technicians and are left brained. They deal with formulas, metrics, and strength of materials. The challenge is to develop their right brains, which deal with empathy and genuine concern for others.

We have generally assumed that our best leaders are our smartest leaders–the smarter the person is, the better leader he will be. In "Social Intelligence and the Biology of Leadership" (*Harvard Business Review*, September 2008, 78–79), Daniel Goleman and Richard Boyatzis propose that the best leader may not be the one with the highest intelligence quota (IQ), but rather the person with the highest "social IQ," or social intelligence.

Leading effectively is achieved by developing a genuine interest in and talent for fostering positive feelings in the people whose cooperation and support you need. It is not about mastering social situations or social skill sets.

If we are going to improve our project managers' emotional and social competency, we must focus on their right brains or soft skills. The right brain focuses on empathy and genuine concern for others. Are you a socially intelligent leader? Goleman and Boyatzis have developed the following Emotional and Social Competency Inventory:

Emotional and Social Competency Inventory
- Empathy – are you sensitive to others' needs?
- Attunement – do you listen attentively and think about how others feel?
- Organizational awareness – do you appreciate the culture and values of the group?
- Influence – do you persuade others by appealing to their self-interests?
- Developing others – do you coach and mentor others with compassion and personally invest time and energy in mentoring?

- Inspiration – do you articulate a compelling vision, build group pride, and foster a positive emotional tone?
- Teamwork – none of us is as smart as all of us. Do you engage the individual members of your team?

You can score yourself by allowing five points per category. How did you score? If you are above twenty-five, your social IQ is pretty good. If you are between fifteen and twenty-five, you now have workable goals. If you are below fifteen, you need to take a hard look at yourself. Maybe your value system needs some adjustment. It is not about you.

The Power of Compliments and Gratitude

The Holy Grail of this chapter, and maybe the entire book, is to be a member of the Compliment-a-Day Club. The Compliment Club was first coined by George W. Crane, a famous psychiatrist, teacher, and author (Dr. George W. Crane's radio talks, 1954). He started using the Compliment Club in 1920. At Bowen Engineering, we still use it today. I guess you can say that good ideas live forever.

Crane was teaching his college class and made an assignment. Each student was to give three compliments every day for thirty days. At the end of the period, the student was to submit a report on the impact the compliments had on 1) the receiver and 2) the student.

I do this in my Leadership and Advanced Project Management class that I teach at Purdue. The reports are astonishing. The students report that they thought the assignment was a little trite at the start, but after they completed the exercise, they thought it improved communications and relationships and changed their outlook on life. Several students commented that they will continue this practice for the rest of their lives.

Every member of the Bowen Engineering family is expected to give at least one compliment every day. If you are not at work, you must compliment someone at home, with something like, "Hey, sweetie, nice dinner!" or "Hey, sweetie, you really look great today."

Our project superintendents are also expected to be a member of the club. Howard McClanahan is one of our top superintendents. He told me a story about the time he complimented his operating engineer who was driving a hydraulic excavator. The operator told

McClanahan that he had been doing this work for twenty years and that was the first compliment he had ever received on the job.

In the class I teach at Purdue, the homework assignment for the first session is to write a letter to your mentor. Half of the class writes to their parents. "Hey, Dad," they may say, "I have never thanked you for your guidance and leadership and for helping me make good decisions for my future."

How easy can it be to have that positive attitude?

Do you think the Compliment-a-Day Club can impact your attitude and your social intelligence inventory? I am a member of the Compliment-an-Hour Club. It has truly helped me grow as a leader.

In *It's Your Ship: Management Techniques from the Best Damn Ship in the Navy* (New York: Grand Central Publishing, 2006, 152), Captain D. Michael Abrashoff says, "I build myself up by strengthening others and helping them feel good about their jobs and themselves. When that happens, their work improves, and my own morale leaps."

I guess the so-called soft side of business is not so soft after all.

Lessons Learned

- Be a member of the Compliment-A-Day Club.
- The only way to be more enthusiastic is to consciously change your behavior.
- It takes courage to be an energy giver.

9

INTRODUCTION TO PROJECT PLANNING

"Planning doesn't happen absent leadership."
– Dave Pedersen, Bowen Engineering board member and
president of Sage Inc.

I n 1980, we started an in-house training program
for foremen and superintendents. We used the
Supervisory Training Program (STP) provided by the Associated
General Contractors of America (AGC). The AGC provides
student manuals and instructor manuals to be used in the classroom.
The AGC also provided instructor training, which I attended. The
current STP is broken into six modules, each of which addresses a
specific area of construction.

At Bowen, we were studying a unit on project management,
and a couple of chapters were devoted to preplanning. We were
astonished that construction companies were planning for
their projects at this level. We implemented the STP program
immediately and still use it today, in modified form. Bowen
Engineering is considered the leader in planning for small- to
medium-sized construction companies, and we have taught the
planning section of the AGC Project Manager Institute since 1990.
Interestingly, that preplanning material was developed by Mike

Casten and Dave Pedersen, who have been management consultants to Bowen Engineering for twenty-five years. Pedersen serves on our board of directors.

Planning is a process. It is a step-by-step breakdown of the project and development of a program for building success. But more importantly, planning is an important part of the Bowen Engineering culture. It defines our company. Our clients recognize us for our project planning. It's all about the customer.

Before you start planning a project, you must ask yourself, "What do we want to accomplish?" What are your goals? What do you want people to say about your job when it is finished? What is your vision? Below you will find Bowen Engineering's corporate project vision.

Project Vision
- Did we delight the client?
- Did we improve margin?
- Did we finish the job early?
- Did we have a safe jobsite?
- Did we develop a project management team?
  - Did we develop staff?
  - Did we improve communications?
- Did we have fun?

Did we delight the client? This question is simply the most important item on the list. If you don't delight the client, you don't deserve to make a profit. Every employee in our company is responsible for client satisfaction, even the lowest laborer. We have clients that only hire Bowen Engineering because we take care of our clients. Client satisfaction is part of the planning process.

Did we improve margin? Doug Bowen meets with every project manager and operations manager quarterly, to discuss each project. The first question asked is, "How can we improve margin?" You don't improve it by cheating subcontractors and vendors; you do it by using planning and ingenuity. Many of our young project managers want to "meet" the budget. No! The question should be, "How do we *beat* the budget?"

Did we finish the job early? How important is it to finish early? The savings in jobsite overhead alone can be substantial. And conversely, when a job goes over the estimated time, what is the first item in the loss column? Jobsite overhead. Early completion will also delight the client.

Did we have a safe jobsite? A safe jobsite can be the difference between success and failure in today's construction industry. Having a fatality can put you out of business, not to mention the anguish it creates for all parties. On our bigger jobs, we have a trailer devoted to safety. It has twenty-eight stations. A new employee spends four hours in safety orientation. We plan our safety program for each project. We usually have a project safety manager who participates in the planning.

Did we develop the project management team? This question is the Holy Grail of planning. There is no better way to develop leadership skills than through the planning process. It brings your team together, assigns them responsibility and accountability, and best of all, it breaks down the wall between the field and the office (we all know that wall exists).

Did we have fun? Is it important to have fun? Is it important that your employees love working for your firm and for you? Do you think that having fun improves productivity? Sure it does. There is that positive attitude again, that we talked about in chapter eight.

We discovered the planning process through the AGC Supervisory Training Program (STP) in 1980. STP at the time came in ten modules. The units we used are now out of print and have been updated more than once. The STP is available for in-house training through AGC of America.

The 1980 version of STP has broken the planning process into fourteen steps. We have expanded the list to include presentations to senior management and the client (*). The important thing is that preplanning is a process.

Preplanning Steps
1. Assign key personnel
2. Preplanning schedule
3. Initial brainstorming session
4. Budget estimate review
5. Procure long lead materials early
6. Visit the jobsite
7. Equipment and manpower requirements
8. Production budgeting

9. Initial construction schedule
10. Subcontracts and purchase orders
11. Preconstruction meetings
12. Final project schedule
13. Organize material handling
14. Final brainstorming session
15. Presentation to senior management *
16. Presentation to client *

You may have a different list. That is not a problem. You should develop the steps that best fit your company. Most of the steps are self-explanatory.

In step two, our planning team develops a preplanning schedule and submits it to senior management. The presentation to senior management has several benefits. Senior management gains confidence that we have a good plan and it gives them an opportunity to share experiences that may help the team. The management team gains visibility with upper management and gets public speaking experience. The savvy project manager will let the superintendent and foremen do the talking. There is no better way to develop leadership skills than through public speaking. Remember, part of our vision is to develop staff.

At Bowen Engineering, we use the following standard preplanning presentation agenda which the teams follow:

Preplanning Presentation Outline
1. Project team – Organization chart
2. Bid results
    a. List of bidders
    b. Overhead and profit forecasts
3. Scope of job
4. Safety – Identify safety hazards
5. Site plan
6. Quality – How will the owner measure it?
7. Project schedule
    a. Completion date
    b. Milestone dates
    c. Liquidated damages
8. Operation plans

9. Procurement
    a. Buy sheet
    b. Gains and losses
10. Opportunities – Where can we improve margin?
11. Challenges
    a. What can go wrong?
    b. What is the biggest risk?
12. Change orders and claims
    a. How are change orders managed by the owner?
    b. What is claim procedure?
13. Team project goals
    a. Completion date
    b. Profit projection
    c. Safety goals
    d. Staff development
    e. Owner relations and communications
    f. How often do we meet with the owner?

We then make the same presentation to our client, although we may not discuss profit with them. The client gains the confidence that we will do a good job, and they also get to meet the management team. This is also an opportunity for us to be in front of our client. We are recognized by our clients for our preplanning presentations.

In the planning process, we try to plan the first two months of the project in great detail. The benefits are definition of the course and flow of the project, development of team solidarity, and insurance of a successful project.

What kind of manager are you? Do you make a commitment to regularly stop all activity and plan the future of the project with the entire management team, or do you work harder, stay later, and run more projects? The choice is yours. When I worked in California, I ran a myriad of projects without an administrative assistant or staff and thought how smart I was.

Bowen Engineering is trying to build an organization and that requires teamwork. The planning process has been a revelation. Our employees will not start a project without doing the preplanning. It has helped develop leaders. It has truly broken down that wall between the field and the office. We have prospered because we have developed a planning culture.

There is no question that if you stop the work and do the planning, you will improve productivity, job costs, completion schedule, customer satisfaction, and safety. I guarantee it. Dr. Emol A. Fails, PhD, FMI Corporation, said, "If you don't know where you're going, you are already there."

Lessons Learned

- There is no better tool than preplanning to develop leadership skills.
- Preplanning is a process.
- Preplanning is a culture.
- Preplanning presentations to senior management are a valuable part of the process.
- Preplanning presentations to our clients also are a valuable part of the process.

10

LEAN CONSTRUCTION – SQP

"Our mission is to transform the experience of project work from frustration and conflict to one of trust and mutual respect."
– Greg Howell, chairman, Lean Construction Institute

According to the US Department of Commerce, productivity in the construction industry has gone down 25 percent in the last fifty years, while productivity in the industrial sector has improved by over 100 percent during the same period (Fig. 1). In 2009, you could purchase a new Volkswagen Jetta for $17,515. In 2017, you could purchase a new Volkswagen Jetta for $17,835. If you consider that the 2017 Jetta had a lot more technology advancements, the price didn't go up at all. Workers at Volkswagen are more productive every year.

You cannot make that same comparison in the construction industry. In construction, productivity is going down every year and construction prices are continuing to escalate. This is a problem for the construction industry, but at the same time, it is an opportunity for those contractors who are willing to take ownership of the situation and do the hard work of improving productivity.

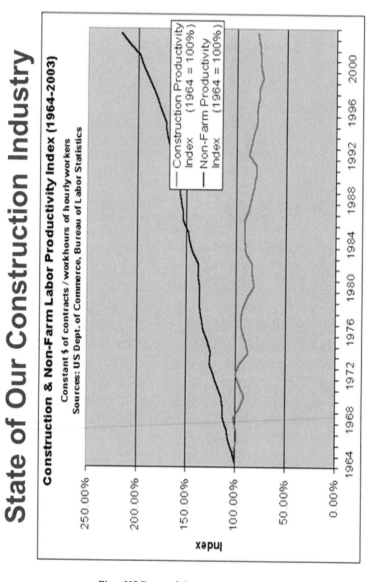

Fig. 1 US Dept. of Commerce graph

At Bowen Engineering, we have just completed the largest single contract in our company's history, the Southport Wastewater Treatment Plant in Indianapolis. The owner, Citizens Energy Group, took over ownership and operation of the treatment plant from the city of Indianapolis in 2011. Bowen's contract will end up at $100 million. That is the good news. The bad news is that we were more than 10 percent low on the original bid and had to beat out our toughest competitor in Indianapolis. For those who know the construction industry, that is impending disaster. A contractor who is 10 percent low will struggle to make a profit. The bigger question was, how much money were we going to lose?

The project is now complete and we actually beat our original budget and finished the work almost a year ahead of schedule. Citizens Energy is delighted with the project, our management team, and the quality of our work. Does it get any better than that? Well, it does. We won the Build America Award from AGC of America for the top utility project in the US in 2016.

In terms of over achievement, it is arguably the most successful project in our company's history. I asked Alan Dale, Bowen project manager, how we could build such a wonderful and successful project. What was the defining difference? His answer was SQP. SQP is our version of Lean Construction. It stands for Safety, Quality, and Productivity.

One of the more interesting parts of the Southport job was a set of ten rectangular dual clarifiers. We had to dismantle the existing sludge collectors and replace them with new equipment. Each clarifier was 41 feet wide, 265 feet long, and twenty feet deep. After we had completed the first clarifier (10 percent of the work), we had spent 22 percent of our budget. At that rate, we would have lost $2 million on the entire operation.

Through Lean productivity improvement, however, we finished the operation on budget. And what was supposed to take eighteen months to complete was completed in only eight months. Through continuous improvement and elimination of waste, we made many changes, including reducing our crew from ten to eight men.

Another critical operation on this project was pouring concrete walls for eight 150-foot diameter circular clarifiers. The walls were 16 feet high and 12 inches thick. The plan was to pour each clarifier in five pours, for a total of forty pours. The objective was to make a pour every day.

It took us ten hours for our first setup. Obviously, we would not pour every day at that rate. Using the Lean productivity improvement process, including step-level planning and continuous improvement, we reduced the setup time to 3.5 hours. We were then able to pour every day, without using overtime.

What is Lean?

The Lean concept comes from the Toyota Production Systems (TPS), which is a system of improved production efficiency. Jeffery Liker captured TPS in his book, *The Toyota Way* (2004). The Toyota Way is the culture that is instilled in every team member at Toyota, helping them to follow and improve the Toyota Production System every day.

What makes it work?
- Philosophy – creating value not making money
- Process – eliminating waste
- People – respect, challenge, and grow them
- Problem Solving – continuous improvement

Lean Construction is an adaptation of the Toyota Production System to fit our unique industry. Just as in manufacturing, Bowen Engineering has seen the need to create the culture to sustain Lean Construction and develop SQP, which our team members live by every day.

AGC of America provides the following definition for Lean Construction in its *Lean Construction Education Program (*Unit 1, page v*)*: "Lean Construction is driven to minimize costs and maximize value on each project completed, challenging all stakeholders to develop and apply better ways to manage the overall construction process." The overarching goal is to eliminate workers waiting for work and work waiting for workers (Unit 3, page 1-1).

Lean is a culture. It is the way we live and operate. Our planning is driven by customer needs and expectations. Everything we do relates back to the customer. That is why as part of our planning process, we do client presentations.

For Lean to be successful, it must be embraced by senior management. But it is also an individual journey. Lean construction is driving accountability to the work face. That can only be done through planning. We are trying to drive leadership to the most junior member of our management team. This means engaging the foremen in planning operations. This approach makes sense because the foreman is the expert director at the workface. He is the craftsman that knows more about the tricks of the trade than the project manager.

It takes a strong team to build any project. The superintendent and project manager provide the leadership to drive success at the work face with the craft. But Lean is a collaborative effort. Planning is most effective when performed as a team, to ensure 100 percent buy-in by all parties. Members of a good team will hold each other accountable for safety and productivity. This also breaks down that invisible wall between the field and the office.

The Lean Construction Institute has developed the Last Planner® System for production planning and control. It was developed by Glenn Ballard and Greg Howell and documented in 2000. It is defined as "the collaborative, commitment-based planning system that integrates should-can-will-did planning." What "should" happen is defined by the master schedule, "can" it happen is defined by the look-ahead planning boards, and "will" it happen is defined by our weekly work plan based upon reliable promises. Finally, how "did" we do? Here we learn, based upon analysis of percent plan complete and reasons for variance. The Last Planner is the foreman.

The Last Planner System utilizes pull planning as opposed to push planning. Push planning is used in traditional construction. Everything is done in sequence, sometimes called batch and queue. Step two follows step one. In pull planning, you start with the ultimate goal in mind and work backwards. Pull planning emphasizes smaller and repeatable operations, thereby minimizing the chance for variations. The circular walls on the Southport project are a good example of pull planning, so that we could make a pour every day.

Lean Construction Goals:
- Identification of waste
- Elimination of waste
- Constant and continuous improvement
- Communication
- Foreman and superintendent accountability

We must provide a work environment that flourishes with production by minimizing waste. By doing so, we add value to the customer and to the company. In order to minimize waste, we must understand its cause and what it looks like. We must develop operation plans that eliminate waste.

Waste is any step or activity that does not contribute directly to the value of the project. Waste can be non-value added but necessary, or it can also be purely non-value added. Our goal is to eliminate non-value added waste and to reduce non-value added but necessary waste.

An example of waste on a project might be the location of the portable toilet. If the carpenter has to walk one hundred yards to use the portable toilet, that is non-value added but necessary. By relocating the toilet and shortening the walking distance, we reduce the amount of the waste.

Continuous improvement must be constant, not just when there is a problem or an issue. It must be all day, every day, and the superintendent and foreman must buy in to the effort.

Communication is the key to the process. You can't communicate by accident. The entire team must be engaged and the series of meetings delivers the goods.

Dave Pedersen, Bowen board member, says, "The project superintendent is the most important role in our industry. The more we can focus our organization on growing great superintendents and understanding how to support them, the more effective and profitable we will become." The superintendent is the key to the Lean culture. He must hold the foremen accountable and drive accountability to the work face.

For companies and/or management teams that are interested in implementing a Lean culture, the recommended steps are:

- Three-day training
- Story boarding
- Step-level planning
- Daily huddles – Job Safety Analysis
- Make Certain plans
- Planning boards
- End-of-shift meetings
- Weekly team meetings

Three-day Training

The first step toward a Lean culture is a three-day training session. An experienced Lean company should conduct training for those new to the concept. The training can be accomplished in-house. For training, AGC of America provides resources for use by the contractor, as follows:

- *Lean Construction Education Program*:
  - Unit 1 – Variation in Production Systems, 2011
  - Unit 2 – Pull In Production, 2012
  - Unit 3 – Lean Workstructuring, 2012
  - Unit 4 – The Last Planner System, 2013
  - Unit 5 – Lean Supply Chain and Assembly, 2014
  - Unit 6 – Lean Design and Pre-construction, 2014
  - Unit 7 – Problem-solving Principles and Tools, 2015
- *J.E. Dunn Construction Case Study: "Implementation of Lean Construction Practices in Managing Construction Projects."* The case study was published by the AGC Education and Research Foundation (https://www.agcfoundation.org).

The Lean Construction Institute also provides training resources.
Lean Construction Institute, Inc.
1400 North 14th Street, 12th Floor
Arlington, Virginia 22209
(703) 387-3050

LCI training modules include:
- Introduction to Lean Project Delivery
- Target Value Delivery
- Introduction to Last Planner System

This training investment is critical for starting a project on Lean principles.

Story Boarding

The idea of story boarding was originally developed by Disney Imagineering. It has been recreated for the construction industry by Mike Casten and Dave Pedersen. Story boarding is a strategy for brainstorming the project by drawing input from the individual members of the management team through open dialogue and by visualizing and memorializing the dialogue. It is critical that the superintendent be included in the process.

Story boarding involves a three-step process that determines:

- <u>What</u> tasks need to be done
- <u>When</u> each task needs to be done
- <u>Who</u> is accountable

The team first lists all of the activities that need to be done in the planning process. This is normally done on a wall using Post-it® notes (Fig. 2). Don't worry about order, just get out all of the ideas. A word of caution, each subcontract and each vendor purchase order would be a separate activity. You would not have a single activity to write all subcontracts. You simply throw all of the activities on the wall as shown (Fig. 3).

Add the Details

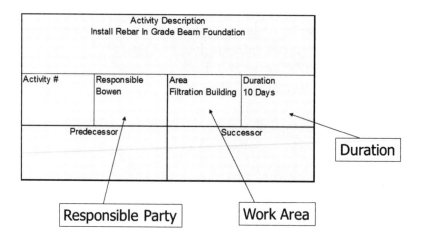

Fig. 2 Post-It notes

Throw Activities on the wall

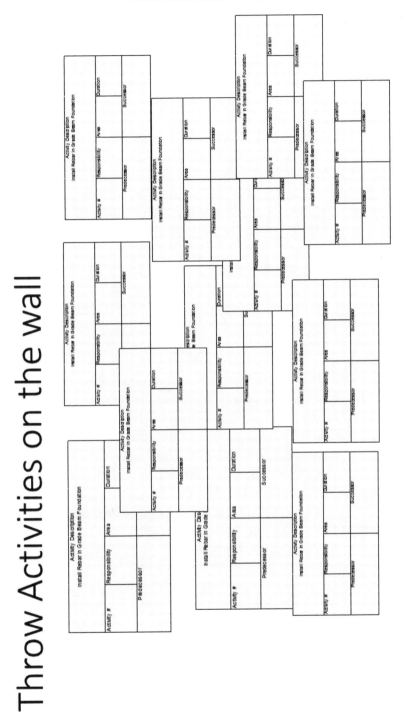

Fig. 3 Post-It notes on wall

The next step is to develop a block schedule or sequence of activities (Fig. 4), putting critical and long lead items in the early weeks. The object is to prevent "show stoppers." Participants then assign responsibility for each task on the Post-it note. The project manager should assign each task responsibility to a member of the project leadership team.

The block schedule will support the development of the project master schedule. The block schedule can be used throughout the project and can help track tasks as they are completed, or not completed. The management team meets every week to go over the story board. The team can add new items, check off items that have been completed, and rebalance the workload as necessary to move the project forward.

Story boarding is a great tool for bringing people together, breaking down that wall between the field and office, and getting input from the entire team. It is also a good tool for punch-list preparation, plant outages, and large or risky operations.

Step-level Planning – Short Step Delay Free

Casten and Pedersen introduced us to step-level planning. The idea is based on the belief that you can improve productivity by factors of two, three, or four times. They call it breakthrough. Instead of looking backward and relying on the accounting department to provide cost reports and bid budgets, we look forward. Throwing out historical information and preconceived notions, we cast ourselves through time and space to achieve improved productivity. By doing this, we tap the imagination and ingenuity of the entire construction team.

Here we are entering the time element to the preplanning process. This is the final preplanning step and is the pinnacle of the preplanning process. It is especially suited for short duration critical activities. How do we develop the "perfect world" production rate? Basically, it is planning an activity through one cycle with zero waste/delays to see what our maximum potential is for an operation.

This becomes a mini-task schedule, showing workflow. It identifies gaps in resources and allows for resource leveling. It is an excellent communication tool for the operation team and allows for quicker identification of possible delays.

Sequence the Activities

Week 1	Week 2	Week 3	Week 4

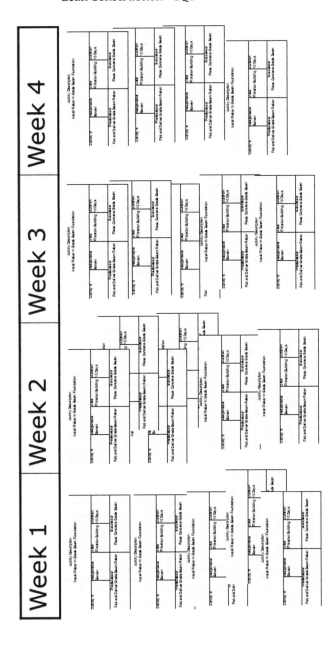

Fig. 4 Block schedule

Step-level planning is a process of breaking an operation down into one-minute to fifteen-minute increments, depending on the duration of the operation. The entire team analyzes each step of the operation with the focus on reducing the overall cycle time. The end product is a visual and user-friendly Gant chart. The process identifies the time which the crew has to complete the operation and individual crew responsibilities. It was especially applicable to our Southport circular clarifier concrete operation because we had fifty repeatable pours.

The example of a step-level plan is from a wall gang forming operation in Owensboro, Kentucky (Fig. 5). On this project, we had fifty repeatable wall pours. In the office, our team thought we could get the crane cycle time down to fourteen minutes as shown. On site, we actually got the cycle time down to eight minutes. Through team engagement and stopping the work process, we were able to obtain magnificent results.

The process also includes resource leveling. At the bottom of the step level plan, you will see the crew members broken down into one-minute increments. This allows you to analyze each crew member to identify inactivity and reassign the person for more efficient productivity.

Beginning-of-shift Huddle

Within the Lean culture, every crew conducts a beginning-of-shift huddle. The huddle is led by the craft foreman. The agenda should include safety, quality, and productivity for the day's activity. This is pretty standard for most companies. For Bowen Engineering's part, when we started daily huddles, our safety metrics began to improve. Once again, we are driving accountability to the workface. This also develops the foreman's leadership skills. A written Job Safety Analysis (JSA) is required for each huddle. This is developed in chapter seventeen.

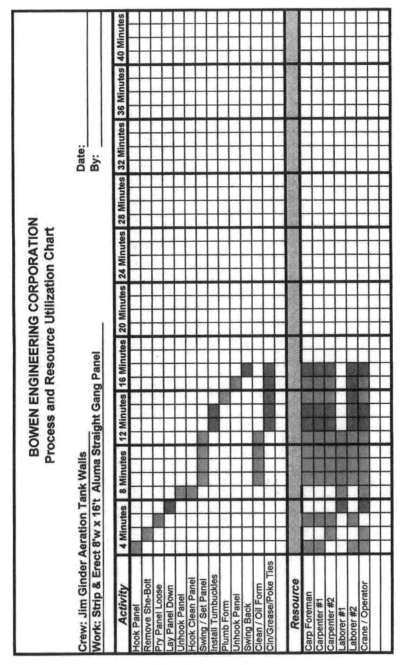

Fig. 5 Step-level plan

Make Certain Plans

The Make Certain plan is developed for each operation that will occur the following week (Fig. 6). This is the responsibility of the foreman. He may get some help the project engineer. His team cannot get on next week's work schedule until he has finished the Make Certain plan. How important is the Make Certain? We are building a $225 million addition to the Petersburg Station for the Indianapolis Power and Light Co. We have employed a full-time project manager dedicated to managing Make Certains.

The Make Certain plan generally has seven elements. We identify these elements with the acronym TIMMESS:

- Time
- Information
- Material
- Manpower
- Equipment
- Safety
- Space

A key part of the Make Certain is identifying minimum work zone expectations. Is the workspace ready to start our operation? Is the site clean? Has the previous activity completed their work and moved on?

Planning Boards

The overall control of the Lean process is the four-week look-ahead schedule. At Bowen Engineering, we do this planning on hard fiber planning boards. Every Bowen project has a trailer dedicated to planning. The planning boards are lined up along one wall, with one board representing each week. When the work for the first week ends, the board for that week is moved to the back of the line. The moved board becomes the fourth week in the look-ahead schedule. Our superintendent, John Eastes, designed rollers to move the boards. His contribution shows how serious everyone is about the planning process. Even adding rollers to planning boards is part of continuous improvement.

MAKE CERTAIN/OPERATION PLAN CHECKLIST			
Bowen			

Bowen Project / Job No.:

Date:

Operation:

Operation Plan Developed by :

Operation Plan Reviewed by :

DESCRIPTION - FLOW OF WORK (STEP LEVEL , SKETCH, NARRATIVE, ETC.):

PRE-REQUISITE WORK REQUIREMENTS / MINIMUM WORKZONE EXPECTATIONS:

Item #	Resp	Complete	Make Certain Task
1			
2			
3			
4			
5			
6			
7			
8			

MATERIAL NEEDED AS A GROUP

Item #	Resp	Complete	Make Certain Task
1			
2			
3			
4			
5			
6			
7			
8			

SAFETY ITEMS

Item #	Resp	Complete	Make Certain Task
1			
2			
3			
4			
5			
6			
7			
8			

MATERIAL NEEDED AS AN INDIVIDUAL

Item #	Resp	Complete	Make Certain Task
1			
2			
3			
4			
5			
6			
7			
8			

TOOLS:

Item #	Resp	Complete	Make Certain Task
1			
2			
3			
4			
5			
6			

MANPOWER & OTHER CREW NEEDS:

Item #	Resp	Complete	Make Certain Task

Fig. 6 Make Certain list

Typical Jobsite trailer

End-of-shift Meeting

At Bowen Engineering, the end-of-shift meeting is held on company time and is led by the project superintendent. The meeting is attended by all foremen, project engineers, and area superintendents. During the meeting, we discuss the day's events and what to expect tomorrow. It is a time when everyone is held accountable for their particular operation. The Make Certain plans and the planning boards are the resource materials for the end-of-shift meetings.

Southport pipe cable support - Indianapolis, Indiana - 2015

Weekly Team Meetings

Bowen Engineering's weekly team meeting is led by the project manager. This is the most important event of the week for the project manager. Here he monitors and confirms completion of the week's activities. The key to the Lean culture is driving accountability to the foreman; getting him to take responsibility, provide leadership, and plan the work. He is the expert.

Here is where we evaluate how we did. The Last Planner System utilizes the percent plan complete (PPC), which is completed weekly assignments divided by total weekly promised assignments. This works very well for a construction manager who has many subcontractors. At Bowen, being a self-perform contractor, we focus on man hours. How many man hours did we work against allotted man hours and time?

How far out should the management team focus? We suggest the following:

- Foreman - two weeks
- Superintendent - two months
- Project manager - two to four months

It is the project manager's responsibility to drive accountability to the foreman and superintendent. By doing this, he now has time to plan for the future and deal with long-range problems.

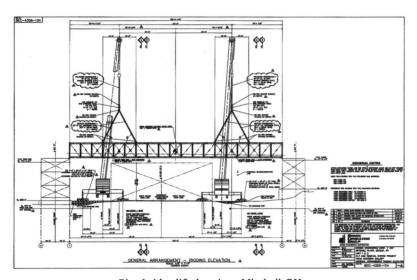

Pipe bridge lift drawing - Mitchell, OH

Modular pipe bridge over major federal highway - Mitchell, OH

At Bowen Engineering, we had a $35 million project in Mitchell, Ohio for the American Electric Power Co. The project went very well and our superintendent Cecil Crawford sent an email around to the entire company, acknowledging a successful pipe bridge that we had built across a major highway. In the email, he praised the crew by name and also credited the management staff that backed him up in the process. It was a celebration. When a superintendent takes that level of interest in the company's success, you have something special.

Crawford hired on at Bowen eleven years ago as a pipe fitter. He had never been a foreman. Crawford moved on to run a $55 million labor-only project for Kansas City Power. It was also successful. He is now a stock holder. How does someone with that background achieve such a wonderful success story? Lean! Foreman engagement and nurturing. This is a dramatic illustration, but we see others like it throughout the company.

What does Lean provide to the project manager, superintendent, and foreman?

- Career development/advancement
- Salary and bonus
- Life/work balance
- Professional relationships and project teamwork
- Pride in performing at the highest level

At Bowen, we want every employee to have the opportunity to do an outstanding job.

What does Lean provide to the company?

- Become the industry's most sought-after company
  - Zero injuries
  - Zero defects
  - Most professional
  - Most innovative and proactive
  - Most trusted
- Grow the organization and careers of valuable employees
- Competitive advantage
- Actual profits exceed bid profit

Here we are. The construction industry is losing productivity. We have the Lean process that could change the industry. The concept has been around for over twenty-five years. It is astonishing to me that only a very few contractors are using Lean. Contractors think they are saving money by reducing staff, when the reverse is true. They save money by developing staff. Beating the supervision budget is not a company objective. It takes courage and management staff to invest in the Lean process, but the payback is enormous.

Successful project management. You make the choice. Make the commitment to regularly stop all activity and plan the future of the project with the entire management team, or work harder, stay later, and run more projects.

Lessons Learned

- Lean construction is a culture. It is the way we do business.
- The key to Lean is foreman engagement.
- Four-week planning boards are the standard for Lean. You cannot get on the board until you have completed your Make Certain plan.
- Utilize step-level planning.
- Utilize story boarding.

Acknowledgements:

I relied on Bowen Engineering team experts Dave Pedersen, Jeff Purdue, Aaron Purdue, Alan Dale, Matt Gentry, and Lacy Wargel to put this chapter together. I could not have completed the chapter without their help and leadership. Thank you very much.

11

MARKETING

*"Marketing is everyone's job; that is why marketing is
everything and everything is marketing."*
– Regis McKenna, chairman, Regis McKenna, Inc.

Wertrated our company in 1967 as a low-
bid public works contractor. We added a marketing
department in the late 1980s, led by Tom Greve. Having a
marketing program seemed like a good idea, and Greve was a
very good salesman. But I don't think we initially embraced the
marketing effort. We were all of the "low-bid" mentality.

Our first real break in the private market came in Danville,
Illinois in 1990. We submitted a bid on a water treatment plant
expansion for the Interstate Water Company. Our low bid was $14
million, but the owner's budget was only $11 million. Through
value engineering, we reduced the price to $11 million, and signed a
contract. The job was a great success.

More importantly, we developed a great relationship with the
owner's chief engineer, Steve Himmell. With Greve's enthusiasm,
Jed Holt's operational skills, and certainly the client's support from
Himmell, we built several water treatment plants throughout the
state of Illinois, all design-build. We knew we were moving into the
private market and we were excited. The work went beautifully. We
had a great partnership with Interstate, but we didn't know how
to take it on the road and expand the private market. We thought

that a good opportunity had simply fallen into our laps and that we needed to continue to be low bidders.

The real turning point came in late 1995. One of our competitors in the water and wastewater business started building intake structures for the power industry. No bids, all negotiated. That came as a big surprise and we decided to look into the situation. Jim Ankrum, one of our senior project managers, set up an appointment with Mark Foster at Cinergy and took me with him.

As a result of that meeting, we were invited to bid on the Cinergy Gas Conversion Project in Noblesville, Indiana. The owner broke the project into packages and we were low bidder on every package. The job was a huge success because of the great partnership formed between Cinergy and Bowen. Our project manager was our future CEO, Doug Bowen.

It only gets better. The owner was so happy with our work that we were invited to bid on their Gibson Station FGD Project near Evansville, Indiana. Once again, we were low bidder. However, this time, Cinergy's management team at the Gibson Station did not want to use us because we were an unknown. Cinergy's upper management, most notably Mark Foster, advocated for Bowen because of the very successful Noblesville project. They prevailed and we were awarded the job.

The project was a total success. The owner's team was led by Bob Ellis, Randy Findlay and Gary Etolen. They were a model of owner leadership and cooperation. They sought our input during the design phase and they sat in on our planning meetings. This drove a culture of mutual trust and respect between the owner, designer, and Bowen. The owner's team was instrumental in building a true integrated team culture. Cinergy's original budget for the project was $40 million. Our final cost came in $14 million under budget. We even earned a bonus for the project.

We learned the importance of everyone working together. I think this is when we started to develop a true marketing culture.

At first, Bowen Engineering didn't understand the importance and value of marketing. It took the Cinergy projects to bring the concept home. If you look at our revenue graph (Fig. 1), we experienced exponential growth beginning in 2000. Much of that growth was due to a serious marketing effort. If we had not developed the marketing culture, our company would be a skeleton of what it is today, or we might not even be in business.

Today, we have a marketing team. But it is not a department or a function, it is a culture. It defines how we do business.

Most construction companies are a commodity. They make their sales based on low price. A public works contractor has to be low bidder. If you are buying a new car and want to pay the lowest price, you shop Ford or Toyota. If you want top quality, you shop for a Cadillac or Mercedes. You can make the argument that you get more value from Cadillac and Mercedes.

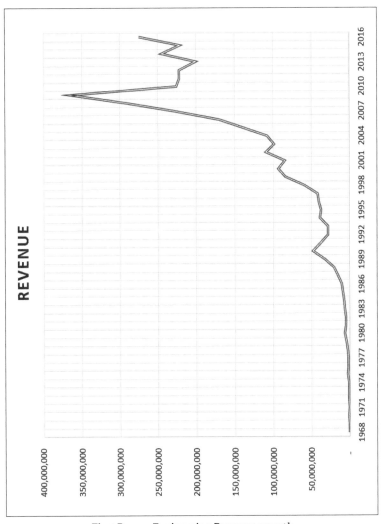

Fig. 1 Bowen Engineering Revenue growth

At Bowen Engineering, we want to be the top-quality producer. Our goal is to provide value-added service to our clients; more than they expect. We do not want to be a commodity.

When I studied at Harvard, we talked about purchasing drivers. In the twentieth century, owners made their purchasing decisions based on low price. In the twenty-first century, they will make their purchasing decisions on relationships. Owners are looking at the intangibles rather than low price. They want timely completion, good communications, and quality work. They don't want claims filed by their contractors. They want to know what the final price of the project will be before the work begins.

How does a contractor sell intangibles? He does it by building a good reputation and providing value-added service. He builds a reputation for quality work and excellent customer service. The best marketing your company can do is to do great work.

How do you sell customer service? It has to be a company culture. Mark Bowell, TESCO Inc., says it best: "Everyone is a salesman."

We do a lot of work in Muncie, Indiana on the city's combined sewer overflow system. The city recently awarded a major expansion project to Bowen Engineering. Our project superintendent is Howard McClanahan and our underground superintendent is Danny King.

When we lay a sewer down a city street in Muncie, our superintendent calls on all of the local residents and business owners and gives them the schedule, tells them what will be involved and when the street will be back in service. We have received many letters of commendation from local residents. Naturally, the city loves our company, but more importantly, they love our superintendents. I am certain that we would not have been awarded the big project if it had not been for the excellent work of our two superintendents. Everyone is a salesman.

There are two goals of marketing:

- Retain existing clients
- Identify and promote new clients

Building personal relationships is the key to retaining existing clients and it starts with people. Solid business relationships involve:

- Trust
- Commitment

- Friendship
- Team spirit
- Character

How do we build relationships? First, we must understand that we are in the personal service business. In our business, personal relationships are critical. It takes more than concrete. Where would we be if we didn't have personal relationships with Steve Himmell at Interstate Water in Illinois, Randy Findlay with Cinergy, or Brad Talley with the City of Lafayette?

In the class I teach at Purdue, Al Oak, president, Cripe Engineering and Mark Bowell, TESCO, teach a session on networking. The material in this section comes from their presentation.

Personal relationships are key to getting and keeping clients. If you aspire to leadership in the construction industry, it will require skills in developing personal relationships. A skill that helps develop personal relationships is networking.

Networking means getting out in the industry and spreading your name and getting to know people. Who are these people? They are owners, design engineers, vendors, subcontractors, and anyone associated with our industry. Be involved in the community such as the chamber of commerce or professional development organizations. My son in law, met his wife, my daughter, when they were on an AGC committee together. You never know where that next contact will take you.

You develop a line of communication and trust by getting to know the person. This requires face to face interaction. This is dominated by body language and attitude. We saw that in chapter eight. Never pass up an opportunity to meet with your client. You build up trust by putting others first. Once again, it is leadership. It is not about you.

Building relationships and networking is a life-long and career-long journey. Don't wait until you have time. Reach back to old relationships. The project manager on the San Luis Canal in California, Kyrk Reid, with Kiewit Construction, taught one of my classes at Purdue. Bill Brown, president of Kaweah Construction taught one of my classes.

The key to success is embracing the importance of personal relationships and making the effort to network. You cannot do this in front of your computer or buried in your iPhone. How does a person get started? Oak says get a mentor. Find someone with a little gray hair and get some pointers. But most important, be intentional with people, it will always pay off.

All construction companies should have a champion for each of their major clients. This person is responsible for developing trust and friendship and ensuring that the firm delivers the goods. He should monitor the job and stay in touch with the client. If the firm drops the ball, he must pick it up and correct any problems. When it comes to team spirit, well, there is that positive attitude again. Character is driven by good values. Our CEO, Doug Bowen, has carried forward the core values that we developed thirty-five years ago.

Being involved in the design phase of the project, or as early as possible, is also one of our goals. The Construction Industry Institute (CII) has developed a curve showing cost versus involvement (Fig. 2). The earlier a contractor is engaged on a project, the more influence he can have on its cost and quality. In a perfect world, we want to be involved before a pencil is put to paper by the engineering department. Once again, we don't want to be a commodity, we want to be part of the project development team.

Traditionally, marketing included advertising, company brochures, and public relations firms. It was a distinct function within the company. Today, marketing must bring the customer inside the company and put marketing at the center of all operations. We often provide design services through design-build or engineering, procurement, and construction (EPC) contracts. This means that we partner with outside design firms. We must market those firms, too, and work with the ones that embrace the same values that we do. Our owners want one-stop shopping and one point of responsibility.

Marketing today is integrating the customer into the contractor's operations. At Bowen, we spend time with the customer, we make a preplanning presentation before construction begins, and we deliver quality service. We take great pains to delight the client and we deliver on credibility. Our company motto is "Resourceful, Responsive, Results." It goes on all of our printed promotional material.

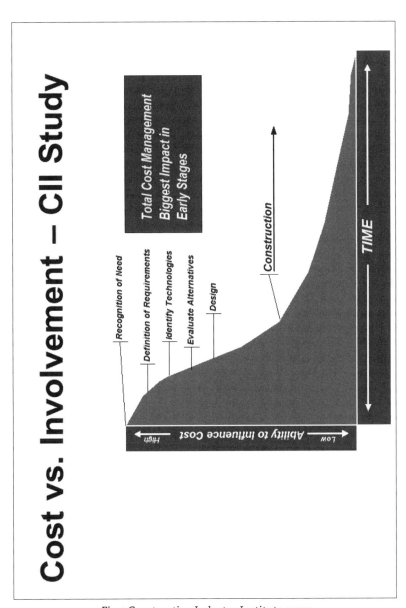

Fig. 2 Construction Industry Institute curve

Credibility is the company's sustaining value. In *The Leadership Challenge*, San Francisco: Jossey-Bass, 2008, 37, authors Kouzes and Posner define credibility as:

- Trustworthiness
- Expertise
- Dynamism

An owner was planning a design-build project. He asked me what the most important consideration is in picking a contractor. I said, "Trust." The owner cannot do design-build absent trust. He has to know that when he goes to bed at night, the contractor isn't back in his office cooking the books.

Expertise sort of goes without saying. You have to know what you are doing. Dynamism, There is that positive attitude again. It keeps cropping up.

How do you delight the client?

- Be punctual.
- Be confident – don't talk in terms of hope.
- Team spirit – have a positive attitude.
- Understand the total scope of the project and the contractor's impact downstream.
- Start with the end in mind – what does the owner consider to be a successful project? Is it based on timely completion or no cost overruns?
- The owner's perception is the contractor's reality.

We started our company building water and wastewater treatment plants in Indiana. In those early years, all of the work for the Indianapolis Water Company was done by Tousley-Bixler, a larger local contractor. We finally broke through the glass wall and were awarded a small chemical treatment building for the Water Company. At our first meeting with the big boss, Ollie Summers, I was late. He was furious. I never did another job for the Indianapolis Water Company until Tousley-Bixler went out of business and Ollie Summers retired.

How a company manages its marketing can be its most powerful form of differentiation. It will determine how a company escapes the "commodity trap." The critical dimensions of a company, including the attributes that define how the company does business, are found in the function of marketing. As Regis McKenna says, "Marketing is everyone's job; that is why marketing is everything and everything is marketing" ("Marketing is Everything," *Harvard Business Review,* 1991).

Lessons Learned

- Building trust is the end game. Everything revolves around trust.
- Everyone is a salesman.
- Marketing defines how a company does business.
- A goal of marketing is to escape the "commodity trap."
- Marketing is not department or function, it is a culture.
- Marketing is founded on personal relationships.

12

GROWING THE BUSINESS

"Nothing improves without change."
– Jeff Purdue, vice president of marketing,
Bowen Engineering

Dynamic growth is essential to business survival. Bowen Engineering has always been on the lookout for new business opportunities. We do this to expand our business, but also to provide opportunities for our talented employees. The cemetery is full of contractors who refused to change.

I attended a business seminar in 1980 put on by the late Leon Danco, former business consultant and president of The Center for Family Business in Cleveland, Ohio. He presented a chart showing three phases of the business life cycle: the work phase, the glory phase, and the problem phase (Fig. 1).

The work phase is certainly difficult. But in total, I think that for Bowen Engineering, it was pretty exciting. The glory phase is when we developed a personality and some permanence. As hard as it is to start a company, the glory phase is more challenging. It is harder to stay on top than it is to get to the top.

The critical phase is the problem phase. According to Danco, that is year number twenty-four. I think it is every year after twenty-four. When a business hits the problem phase, it has to decide if it will grow, hold even, or downsize. A thriving business is continually faced with this kind of choice. I don't think a company can hold even or downsize and still survive. A business enterprise is a living organism or work in process. It has to be fed.

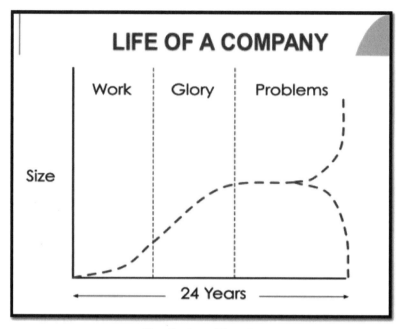

Fig. 1 Business life cycle

Sometimes we make good choices and sometimes we make bad choices. Those choices are made in the good times. So, we have to be careful. Just because we were successful last year does not mean we will be successful this year or next year. Success is not permanent. You have to pay attention every day.

Personal computers came out in the late 1970s. We bought one. We didn't know how to use it. At first, all we did was write letters, and it worked well. Then we purchased a Lotus 123 and we were on our way. The train was at the station. We didn't know where it was going, but we wanted to be on it. That has become our standard operating procedure.

Bowen Engineering has expanded into new markets on several occasions. If we had not done so, we would not be in business today. Or at the very least, we would be a skeleton of what have become. I think it is just a basic business principle that you must grow to survive.

I will share four situations of where we expanded our business. All of these examples fall into the problem era. We did not need to expand. We were rolling along, perfectly happy. We were profitable, building a good reputation, and building quality projects. But we wanted to build a better company. We wanted to be better tomorrow than we were today.

Sewer Business

We hired Bob Newman in 1974. He was a great leader and a great technician. He ran construction equipment for our core business of building water and wastewater treatment plants. But he had been brought up in the sewer business and knew how to lay sewer.

It was a natural evolution that we would think about getting into the sewer business. Most of our public works customers took separate bids on treatment plants and sewer collection systems at the same time. If we had the capability of doing sewer work, we could offer bids on both jobs. If we won both jobs, we could even offer a discount. This would give us a small competitive advantage.

Combined sewer overflow system - Lafayette, Indiana - 2015

To get into the sewer business, we needed an estimator with underground experience. We hired Charlie Fitzgerald from Eagle Valley Construction. He was a perfect fit. We now had an experienced estimator and superintendent. I can still remember the scuttlebutt in the local sewer construction market. With Newman and Fitzgerald working at Bowen, they would be hard to beat.

The sewer business is different from the treatment plant business. There is more risk because you never know for sure what is waiting for you underground. It is hard to get a reasonable return on investment because of that risk. On a plant job, it is generally above ground and you can see what you are dealing with. We were unique. None of our plant competitors got into the sewer business.

We are still building sewer projects today. But our market has changed somewhat. Most of our sewer work falls under our performance contracting umbrella. The sewer business has served us well. It has expanded our skill set and enables us to better serve our customers.

Micro Tunneling

Moving into micro tunneling was taking Bowen's sewer business to the next level. We thought it was an emerging market. We purchased micro tunneling equipment for $1 million and started bidding projects. Our first couple of projects did not go too well. The tunneling portion went well, but it was the ancillary parts like access shafts and open cut sewers adjacent to the work that caught us in our knickers.

We submitted a bid to construct a tunnel in Dayton, Ohio. The tunnel was 48 inch diameter, 1 mile long, running from Dayton to Centerville, under the Centerville Highway. We were $1 million low on a $4 million bid. I wanted to withdraw our bid, but Fitzgerald threatened to quit if we did. I think we failed to reflect a reasonable return on risk in our bid.

The project was in solid rock, so we naturally had a rock bit in our equipment setup and pricing structure. Our tunneling operation was getting thirty linear feet per day, which was close to our estimate. All of a sudden, our equipment ran out of rock and into pure dirt. The rock bit would not dig the dirt. And we were 70 feet below the ground surface. We couldn't pull the drill rig out because the sewer pipe followed the drill rig into the tunnel. It looked like we would have to sink a shaft at the cutting head and either change the cutting teeth or hand mine the remainder of the tunnel. We thought we were looking at a $1 million loss.

Micro tunneling bore pit

After some strategic thinking and soul searching, which included talking to the micro tunneling equipment manufacturer, we attempted to cut the dirt with the rock bit. It worked. I got a call from Jim Ankrum, project manager on the job site. He said the crew covered ten linear feet that day. He called it "warp speed." We soon ran back into rock again and the rest of the job went well. We broke even on the project. Under the circumstances, I think we did well.

Next, we bid a micro tunneling job in Wichita, Kansas. There were ten bidders. We were not low. With that many bidders, I guess you could say this was not much of an emerging market, after all. We decided to close our micro tunneling adventure and sold the equipment for $600,000. That was more than we had in the books, after depreciation. That was the only time we made any money in the micro tunneling business.

We tried micro tunneling. We were not successful, but we didn't lose any money. My sense is that our employees give us good marks for having tried it. Maybe this experience has made us stronger as we try other new business ventures.

Structural Steel Erection

We were working on our second major power plant project at the Gibson Station, just outside of Evansville, Indiana. The owner for our first two power plant projects was PSI, now Cinergy. The job was a wonderful example of teamwork between the owner, the design engineer, and the contractor. Cinergy's Randy Findlay was so impressed with our performance on the Gibson FGD Project, that he approached us. "We need Bowen to add structural steel and boilermaker to your self-perform capabilities. There's no reason you can't be wildly successful adding these services."

Jeff Purdue, senior manager over our Gibson project, put a business plan together and presented it to upper management and the board of directors. The plan included hiring Robert Redden, a veteran ironworker superintendent, who was working on the Gibson Power Plant.

Bowen's board of directors liked the idea, but was concerned about worker's compensation exposure. The ironworkers had the highest worker's comp rate in the construction industry. The board even considered setting up a separate company to avoid any serious accident claims against Bowen Engineering. In the end, the board decided that it was probably too complicated to set up another company, so we decided to move forward.

This strategy expanded our deliverables to our power clients and it opened up doors to larger and more exciting projects. We were now doing steel erection and boilermaker work. It went really well and expanded our market. But one of the biggest advantages was that Redden hired some fantastic ironworker and boilermaker superintendents. These men, Roger Harill, Ebby Benson, and Matt Vaughn, are now building successful projects for Bowen all over the country, and they are stockholders.

Setting gypsum tank with a 230T Manitowoc 888

Installing Ductwork

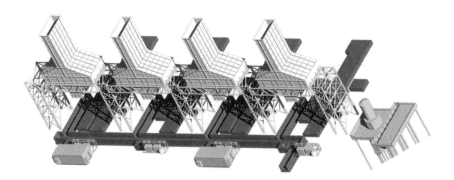

CAD Drawing of SCR

Selective Catalytic Reduction (SCR)

After the Gibson Station project, we picked up our largest work package to date for The American Electric Power Co, at their Clifty Station in Madison, Indiana. Our $75 million bid for the job was time and material with a guaranteed maximum price. We finished the job ahead of schedule and under budget. We would not have won that project if we had not grown our business by starting a steel erection operation.

Adding this facet to our deliverables has had a huge impact on our company. Without it, we would not be half the company we have become. It has expanded our market, grown our company, developed us into a better-managed company, and opened doors of opportunity. Always listen to your customers.

Performance Contracting

Performance contracting is a form of design-build, but it includes some added benefits to the owner. In the Indiana wastewater industry, performance contracting must also provide energy savings or operating savings as part of the deliverables. Owners can select their providers from companies who respond to a request for qualifications (RFQ) or a request for proposals (RFP). They can consider many deliverables in addition to price. Most owners require time and material contracts with a guaranteed maximum price.

Our first performance contracting project was in 2002, on the Bloomington Wastewater Treatment Plant Expansion. We were a subcontractor and only provided the construction services. The financing, project management, and overall project development was handled by another firm. The project went very well and introduced us to performance contracting.

After finishing the project, we felt we could have handled the entire project on our own and did not need an outside firm to provide overall management. This would eliminate double markups and make us more competitive. It would also provide our clients with a lower cost.

Kris Bowen was on our marketing team and got us involved in performance contracting. It was also her idea that we could do the entire project on our own. Thanks, Kris.

We hired Dave Wrightsman and Steve Nutt to run the performance contracting department. Today, Nutt is in charge. We are the leading performance contracting provider for wastewater treatment construction in the state of Indiana.

Nutt is the rain maker. He helps owners develop a performance contracting strategy. Everybody wins, especially the owners. But he gets back-up from our employees. They are all salesmen. They understand that they must support Nutt's marketing effort. Our project managers and superintendents provide excellent service. We work together as a team. Our clients love our entire team.

Owners are tired of claims and poor performance. Performance contracting allows owners to select contractors who will deliver the goods without any problems. Owners also want to know what the final project is going to cost, before it starts.

One of our first clients in performance contracting was the Town of Plainfield, Indiana and their consulting engineer, Butler Fairman and Seufert (the design engineer on our Jamestown project, see chapter three). Both were early adapters and helped to define Bowen's performance contracting process. A quote from a letter written by the Town Engineer, Tim Belcher, says it all.

"I can say without hesitation that over my twenty-five years of contracting experience, I have not had a more satisfying and rewarding public contracting experience. Not only is the performance contracting method superior to other forms of public project delivery, but Bowen's abilities have been innovative, professional and prompt, resulting in excellent project outcomes."

These abilities were delivered by our project manager, Dan Bernath, and his various management teams time and time again. He has implemented multiple water, wastewater and sewer projects over eight continuous years.

Combined sewer overflow system - Muncie, Indiana - 2016

Another one of our early performance contracting customers was the City of Lafayette, Indiana. We had just finished the Lafayette Waste Treatment Rehabilitation for $57 million. The job went very well and we won a Build America Award from AGC. The owner's rep for the project was Brad Talley, Lafayette Utility Superintendent. We had a very good relationship with Brad and moving into performance contracting was a natural evolution. The City Engineer was Jenny Miller Leshney, she was also a good partner.

We have worked with the City of Lafayette for five continuous years. The project manager is Jared Weber and the superintendent is Matt Tafflinger.

While we were working on a sewer project under performance contracting, the City had a sewer emergency on Highway 26 in another part of town. A sewer had collapsed and created a huge cavity in the street intersection. It was a major intersection and occurred on a weekend when Purdue was playing a football game. The City was in a bind.

Bowen immediately stepped in to solve the problem. Chris Manges, project manager and Scott Runion, project superintendent, called in every sewer specialist at Bowen from around the mid-west. We worked twenty-four hour shifts and got the sewer and street intersection back in service, and put the City of Lafayette back in business. We received the following email from Brad Talley.

> *Bob and Doug,*
>
> *I wanted to send a quick note to thank you and your crews for all the work done during Lafayette's emergency repair on 26 and Creasy Lane last week. The guys worked hard and safe and got the job done. I really appreciate the fact that I can call on Bowen and know that the job will get done right. Scott Runion and the entire crew went above and beyond to resolve a very difficult situation.*
>
> *Brad Talley, Lafayette Utility Superintendent*

Brad Talley is a great partner and appreciates quality service, and teamwork. Does it get any better than that? Well it does. This is the email that our CEO, Doug Bowen, sent back to Brad.

> *Brad,*
>
> *We can't pull these kinds of successes off without great clients! We very much appreciate the opportunity to serve you. We will certainly pass along to the gang.*
>
> *Doug*

We built combined sewer overflow systems in Muncie, Indiana and Lafayette, Indiana using the performance contract delivery.

Performance contracting is a partnership between the city, the design engineer, and the contractor. All of the work has gone very well, proving once again that teamwork works every time. The finished sites also enhanced the décor of the city's aesthetics.

Another of our more interesting projects was a $25 million contract to construct a combined sewer overflow system for the City of West Lafayette, Indiana. As part of the project, we were to include roadway reconstruction. Using our construction engineering expertise, we were able to reuse the spoil excavation from the sewer operation to raise the grade of a major and very complicated highway intersection 10 feet.

We eliminated hauling of the spoil material to a disposal area and the import of fill material for the intersection. This resulted in a cost savings for hauling spoil and the purchase and hauling of import fill. The savings to the owner was $2 million.

With the $2 million savings, the owner awarded us a change order for additional work they had contemplated but couldn't afford. Everybody won. It was a job made in heaven. We recycled all spoil material and built a major intersection with free dirt. It proved that when the owner, design engineer, and contractor work together, everybody wins.

To wrap up performance contracting, I will use a quote from Anthony Goodnight, Public Works Director, City of Huntington, Indiana:

> *"The City of Huntington would like to express our appreciation for the improvements Bowen Engineering made at our waste water treatment plant. Being the City's first guaranteed savings contract, Bowen exceeded our expectations and delivered a great project on time and under budget. As a result of the success, the city has continued the use of this contracting method.*
>
> *The team that Bowen assembled to manage this project was exemplary and should be commended. There was never a doubt that the City came first and the team did their best to make sure everybody walked away a winner. We look forward to the next project with Bowen Engineering."*

The project superintendent was Matt Lash, and the project managers were Mark Cvetkovich and Alan Dale.

You have to be imaginative to grow the business. You have to engage your employees and encourage creativity. Few people can do it alone.

As I write this book, I am a little astonished at what we have accomplished. It goes back to creativity, good values and people.

Lessons Learned

- You have to grow to survive.
- You have to give your employees the opportunity to be creative.
- When you expand into a new market, hire someone with market expertise.
- Always be on the lookout for excellent people.

West Lafayette - Roadway redesign - 2015

13
WHAT CAN GO WRONG?

"Don't be too proud to face up to your goofs and improve
your future judgement."
– Mitch Daniels, president, Purdue University

We have made a few mistakes. We have used bad judgement on some of our past jobs. But one of our core values is "We never walk away from a problem". We finished all of those jobs to the satisfaction of the customer. We left the projects with our heads held high.

There is no better teacher than failure. Four projects were a particular challenge to Bowen Engineering. We are a better company today, because of these experiences.

Busseron Conservancy District – 1974

Swifty Oil had a large group of gas stations in southern Indiana. They thought there was easy money in the construction business, so they tried their hand. They immediately picked up two earthen dams for the Bureau of Conservation. They completed the first dam and decided they didn't want to be in the construction business anymore. So, they looked to find another contractor to take over the second dam.

We were approached by Harold Nolan, a dirt mover in Noblesville, Indiana, who had contacts with Swifty. He convinced us to look into the job and consider taking over the contract for

Swifty. This would mean providing a performance bond and then becoming the contractor of record. Swifty's price for the second dam was $200,000.

We worked up a bid for the project, including a price from Nolan to move the dirt. Our price was $250,000 and it was accepted. We thought we had hit the mother lode. How easy could this be? We were now the contractor and started the project.

Nolan had scrapers but he didn't have a dozer. He needed a dozer on the job, and the rental companies wouldn't rent him one. So, we bought a Caterpillar D6 dozer for $30,000 and rented it to Nolan for $1,500 per month. At the end of the job, he could continue to rent the machine or we could sell it.

The job did not go well from the get-go for Nolan or Bowen. Before he was finished with his work, he sued us for $1 million. He said we had put him out of business and to calculate his damages, he figured the loss of income for the rest of his life.

I was devastated. We had been in business less than ten years and if we didn't beat this claim, we were out of business. I did not handle this well. I couldn't sleep, I could barely navigate, and I was totally debilitated from worry. I had never been in a lawsuit before, so I called my cousin, Tom Wood, for advice. He had been in a number of lawsuits. He said, "Don't worry, it's just money."

I also didn't have an attorney, so I called Jack Crane, our outside CPA, for a recommendation. He suggested Tom Withrow. I had played basketball with Withrow and knew him to be a really nice guy. I said "Jack, this is a $1 million lawsuit. I need someone who will kick butt and save my company." He said, "Tom Withrow is the meanest alley fighter in the city of Indianapolis." We hired Withrow and he remained our corporate lawyer for the next twenty years.

To Nolan's credit, even though we were involved in a lawsuit, he finished the work to the last spoonful of dirt. He pulled off the job and took our bulldozer with him. So now, we had a law suit and also a missing bulldozer.

Five years after the suit was filed, we settled with Nolan for $7,500. We found the dozer on a farm in southern Indiana and sold it for $19,000. It was bucket of bolts, but when you have that Caterpillar name on the side, the price goes up. Our lawyer's bill was $20,000.

R.R. Donnelley Water Filtration - 1984

Getting our marketing program going in a low-bid environment was difficult. Tom Greve, marketing director, got us invited to bid on a new water filtration system for the R. R. Donnelley Company in Wabash, Indiana. It was design-build and our only competition was Shambaugh Mechanical in Fort Wayne, Indiana.

It was a pressurized water filtration system. Shambaugh used a single-unit system provided by General Filter, who was the acknowledged leader in the industry. We used a double-unit filtration system using an alternate manufacturer from Birmingham, Alabama. Ours was a relatively new way of providing pressure filtration. Our design partner was out of Columbus, Ohio. The basic system was designed by the manufacturer and our design engineer put the overall project together and stamped the drawings. Two units were housed in a single pressure vessel and separated by a steel diaphragm.

There were four double-unit filters in the project. We installed the tanks per plans and specs and removed the older system, which was being replaced. The units were tested and approved. The owner then placed the system in operation. They only used one filter in the beginning because demand was down at the time.

After the first day, we noticed a crinkle in the tank we had been using. How could you have a crinkle in a high-pressure vessel? We opened the access hatch and discovered that we had crushed the diaphragm. We determined that by using only one filter in a two-unit filter tank, we were creating high pressure in the used filter side and zero pressure in the unused filter side. The pressure differential crushed the diaphragm and deformed a high-pressure vessel. No one had told us that you had to run both filters within a pressure tank simultaneously.

The situation was further complicated by the fact that R. R. Donnelley needed water to run their printing business. If they didn't have clean water and were forced to shut the plant down, their losses would be $1 million per day. And the original system had been taken out of service. If they had to shut down, where do you think they would look for coverage of their losses?

We figured out that you had to run two filters at a time. We changed the controls accordingly and placed the remaining filters into service. It was touch-and-go, but the system worked. Donnelley wondered, and rightly so, if they had bought a lemon. Donnelley never had to shut down and I think we demonstrated that the system would work. They worked with us very nicely, but were plenty nervous.

The manufacturer provided the replacement filter. We removed the failed unit and installed the replacement unit. We also had to redesign the electric controls. Our costs for the correction were $250,000, and I filed a claim against the manufacturer. Our claim was rejected, so we filed for arbitration.

In the process of developing our case, I visited the manufacturer's facilities in Birmingham. The owner offered us $70,000 to settle the claim. I refused and we proceeded to arbitration. Our lawyer's bill was $70,000. Our management time to develop the claim was $30,000, for a total cost of $100,000. The arbitration panel awarded us zero. They said that the blame for the debacle belonged to the design engineer.

Looking back, I have come to realize that I could probably have negotiated with the manufacturer and gotten them up to $100,000. My failure to negotiate and to instead pursue arbitration cost Bowen Engineering $200,000. It proved once and for all that a bad settlement is better than a good lawsuit.

I remember a similar situation in Indianapolis. A local contractor built a building in Ohio. It did not go well and they filed a claim for $2.5 million. The owner offered $1.5 million. The contractor turned it down and sued. The judge awarded $1.5 million to the contractor. His lawyer's bill was $1.5 million. His decision to sue cost him $1.5 million.

My grandfather on my mother's side built homes in Portland, Indiana. He used to say, "When going to court, if you lose, you lose, and if you win, you lose."

Tennessee Valley Authority (TVA) Fly Ash Project – 2008

We had done four projects with TVA under the banner of URS as a subcontractor. The jobs went beautifully. We were profitable and the owner, TVA, was very pleased with our work. All of the work was in the Knoxville area.

In the process of building the jobs, we befriended a local electrician, Miller Electric. Miller was in tight with TVA. We then hired one of their principals who was the major go-between with TVA, thinking that this would help us develop a relationship with TVA.

Miller brought us a lead to remodel the fly ash system at two plants in Knoxville. Our partners would be United Conveyor Corporation (UCC) in Milwaukee, Wisconsin and Mesa Engineering in, Chattanooga, Tennessee. $50 million dollars on the two sites. It was decided that UCC would be the prime on one site and Bowen would be the prime on the other. TVA thought our price was too high and they had us cut out our $1 million contingency. They said that if we needed it, they would add it back in later.

Miller was the electrician. The principal who had just joined our company did most of the electrical pricing, even though he worked for us. The electrical price was too low and was further complicated by the fact that Miller had never done a project of this magnitude. We determined at the half way point in the project that Miller did not have enough money to compete the work.

We did not have a performance bond on Miller. Filing a suit for damages was out of the question since Miller didn't have any resources and had the ear of TVA. One of the projects was smaller, so we had them finish that work, for which we paid additional funds. On the bigger job, we cancelled the Miller subcontract and hired an outside electrical sub. This infuriated the TVA management.

TVA also made a lot of scope changes, including putting over 60 percent of the work in shutdown mode. These changes added cost. We had figured to do the job at our leisure, under no time constraints. Now we had to build most of it in shutdown mode with an accelerated time schedule. Jeff Purdue was over the project for Bowen and did everything possible to get financial relief for the changes. The TVA management not only refused to compensate us for the scope changes, they threatened to cancel our contract and throw us off the job. During the shutdown, they had 400 workers of their own on the site. Whenever there was a conflict, our work was stopped.

Purdue laid his life on the line to do battle on these issues. TVA management, for their part, was upset with Purdue because he was fighting back, as he should have. Their response was to have him physically removed from the job.

Jed Holt then took over the job. The TVA management threatened to report us to the inspector general. Holt said, "Bring them on! We would love to tell the IG how we have been treated." The IG conducted an interview, but nothing came of it.

We went into the job with great expectations and enthusiasm. We had good relations with Miller and TVA. UCC looked like a good partner and Mesa Engineering was local and had worked with TVA, but everything backfired. Certainly, we should not have hired Miller. Today, we prequalify all subs over $1 million. At TVA, we got new management and they turned out to be the owner from hell. UCC did not work out, either. You should never let the equipment manufacturer be the prime contractor. When you lose control of part of the job, you lose control of all of the job.

In spite of these obstacles, we finished the job on time. Because of our superior financial strength, we were able to weather the storm. We filed claims against TVA and UCC and the negotiations were led by our CEO, Doug Bowen. It took over two years and a lot of hard work, but we did obtain some financial relief from both TVA and UCC.

We are a better company today because of our TVA experience. One change we made is that our CEO holds quarterly reviews of every project with the project manager and operating manager. They focus on how to improve margin and identify any potential profit fade.

NRG - Big Cajun SNCR – 2013

We were invited to price a Select Non-Catalyst Reduction (SNCR) process using urea injection in Louisiana. We had just finished an FGD Water Treatment Plant unit at the Conemaugh Station for the same owner, at News Florence, Pennsylvania. It was a $30 million project and went beautifully.

The Louisiana project included water treatment, water distribution, and urea injection. The original scope and estimate was $15 million. The owner purchased all of the equipment and wanted a lump sum contract. We were to provide all construction labor and wiring. The project included a lot of electrical wiring and heat tracing, for which there were no drawings.

NRG was under a consent decree. There were three coal-fired boilers and they all had the same finish date. There were $100,000 per day liquidated damages for the owner.

Senior management wanted to sign the lump sum agreement. But Bill Fyffe, operations manager, refused. He said the job was "unpriceable." Fyffe had just finished a similar project for Dow Chemical in Houston and he wasn't going through that again. Fyffe prevailed and we signed a time-and-material plus fixed-fee contract with NRG.

We worked around the clock, two shifts, seven days per week, for six months. At our peak, we had 700 union workers on site. All work was done on a live plant. The boilers were never shut down. We had to install urea injectors on live lines wearing fire protective suits and the owner compressed the schedule. All of the piping was welded stainless steel. We had great workers and had almost zero weld failures.

The final price came in at $40 million and the owner refused to pay it. We had informed the project people as the price went up, but there appeared to be a breakdown in communications with corporate. Fyffe and Charlie Douglas had prepared a good agreement and we prevailed. NRG paid us all of our costs and the agreed-upon fee. Corporate retaliated. They cancelled two projects we had under contract in Houston and they fired their project manager in Louisiana.

Thank goodness Fyffe had refused to sign a lump sum agreement and Douglas had put together a first-class time-and-material contract. We could easily have seen a $10 million loss. You have to understand risk.

Russell Clough, Stanford University professor, says that even the best contractors in the industry lose money on 10 percent of their jobs. You could argue that we are ahead of the curve. The fact is that the construction industry is dangerous and challenging. Contractors are aggressive and are going to face problems. The test is whether or not we have honored our commitments and learned from our mistakes?

Malcolm Baldridge, United States Secretary of Commerce, once said, "Good judgement comes from experience. Experience comes from bad judgement."

Lessons Learned

- A bad settlement is better than a good lawsuit.
- Don't underwrite your subs and vendors.
- Prequalify all subs.
- Require a performance bond for all subs over $1 million.
- Don't give up control of the project.
- Allow for contingencies on tough work.
- Don't hire managers/leaders from your partners.
- Understand risk.

14

WHAT CAN GO WELL?

"Ain't life grand?"
– Brian Stater, chief public works estimator,
Bowen Engineering

We have certainly had our challenges over
the years. But we have been in business since 1967 and we have
had some pretty neat projects along the way. You couldn't stay in
business if you didn't have some successes. And we have built a fairly
good reputation in the industry. In fact, we have won seven Build
America Awards, presented by the Associated General Contractors
of America (AGC).

Some key projects changed the landscape, so to speak.

Fort Wayne Sewer Demonstration Project – 1971

We bid and won a $1.5 million pump station and screening
structure in Fort Wayne, Indiana. It was the largest project we had
built to that date. We had to beat out C & C Construction, which
was located in Fort Wayne. I had considered C & C for employment
when I returned to Indiana from California. The pump station was
situated on the bank of the Maumee River, and was 50 feet deep by
50 feet wide by 100 feet long.

It was a daunting project. It was a long way from home and
difficult construction, but we were unafraid. We purchased a new
1.5 CY track loader from Allis Chalmers and had just taken delivery
on a brand-new 45 ton Link Belt Crawler Crane.

Our plan was to excavate the hole with the track loader. That was the way we did it in California; pretty cheaply. One machine does the digging and the hauling. We were ahead of budget in the beginning. It was raining and as we approached the bottom of the excavation, the loader couldn't handle the material. It was too deep and too wet for the loader to get the dirt out of the hole.

We decided to sheet the entire bottom foundation, which was not in the bid. We then put a small dozer in the bottom, to loosen the remaining dirt and clam the spoil out of the hole with the link belt. It was slow going and the rainy weather wasn't making it any easier.

We finally finished the excavation, installed the footing forms, and were installing the final rebar. The foundation was 4 feet thick and we scheduled our first pour of 200 CY for a Friday morning. I was in Indianapolis on Thursday and was driving to the jobsite Friday morning. I remember driving up I-69 and it was raining. I can still see the windshield wipers going back and forth. I was terrified.

Pouring concrete - Fort Wayne, Indiana - 1972

We couldn't pour early morning because we still had some forms to buckle up and the inspector wouldn't let us pour because we had some mud on the rebars and a few bars were out of line. We finally started our pour at noon. At 1:30 p.m., Roy Adamson, Bowen superintendent, said "Bowen, we are going on luck alone." We finished the pour at 8:30 p.m. and all went into town to have steaks and beer at the Gas Light. Whew!

When we returned to the job on Monday morning, the banks of the excavation had caved in all around the structure. The sheet piling had fallen over and was resting against the concrete foundation. It took us two weeks to clean up the mud, pull out the sheet piling, re-slope the banks, set up a dewatering system, and get ready for the concrete wall forms. But the concrete was in place.

I am pretty certain that had we not poured the foundation that Friday, you would not be reading this book and would never have heard of Bob Bowen. Henry Bradikis was the project manager for design engineer, H. B. Steeg (now HNTB), and he thought I was a pretty young guy to build a project like this. I agree.

Jeffersonville Water Treatment Plant – 1997

We had built several design-build projects in Illinois for the Interstate Water Company. And we had just completed three design-build projects for the Indiana American Water Company for $15 million. They had gone very well. The Indiana American projects were time and material plus fees for overhead and profit. The owner was very pleased with the projects. HNTB was our design partner.

Indiana American was getting ready to build a brand-new $32 million water treatment plant in Jeffersonville, Indiana. The American Water brass in Vorhees, New Jersey wanted to put the project out for qualifications and proposals to several contractor teams. Eric Thornburg, COO for Indiana American, wanted to use HNTB and Bowen. He felt that the first three projects had gone so well, why change? Thornburg appreciated quality and the wonderful partnership we had formed. He prevailed and we were awarded the job. Thornburg was a true partner and he went out on a limb for Bowen Engineering. He moved on soon after this project was completed, to become the president of the Connecticut Water Company in Hartford, Connecticut.

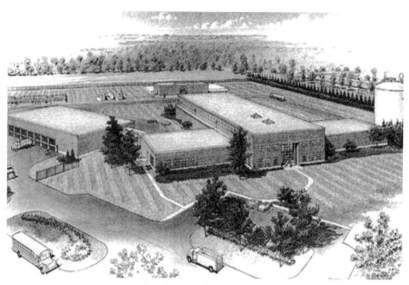

Rendering of plant - 1994

That job became our flagship project. It could not have gone better. I think it was a turning point for Bowen Engineering becoming a real market-driven company. Everyone was on board to do a quality project. Even the laborers were fired up and excited about being on the project. We brought the job in for $26 million, which was $6 million under the original budget.

This is another example of the owner, the designer, and the contractor working together in concert. If you worry about costs, the owner got all of the savings. It was truly a great team.

Indianapolis International Airport Utility Tunnel – 2005

The City of Indianapolis was building a new airport terminal. They needed utility services, but thought they could use an abandoned power/utility plant owned by United Airlines on the north side of the air field. United had at one time run a maintenance facility at the airport, which was now shut down. To accomplish that, they planned to run utility lines under the main runway.

The airport's design engineers had designed a 12 foot diameter walk-through tunnel. Their initial estimate was $48 million. That was way above the Airport Authority's budget and there was also a one-year delay to get a 12 foot diameter tunneling machine. This would delay the opening of the new $1 billion airport terminal.

Tunnel boring machine

Doug Bowen and Dan Liotti of Midwest Mole - 2005

The city approached us to explore alternate solutions. Charlie Fitzgerald, Bowen's sewer estimator, designed a 7 foot diameter tunnel. Our price was $32 million. Not only did we save the city $16 million, but we could get the 7 foot tunneling machine immediately, thereby meeting the Airport Authority's time table. The machine was in demand, so we had to commit to using it before the city gave us a contract. This was a gamble on our part, but it worked out.

We proposed to fill the tunnel with cellular grout with no water. We used galvanized plates to avoid corrosion and the water lines were jacketed to eliminate maintenance. We teamed with Dan Liotti of Midwest Mole. Liotti and Fitzgerald made the initial presentation to the city. Citizen's Thermal was the owner's rep on the project.

There was zero tolerance for any runway settlement. This was monitored very carefully by the Airport Authority. If the airport were to shut down, it would cost the city $1 million per day. Like Fitzgerald said, "If you shut the airport down, you might as well shoot yourself."

The job was a total success. It was delivered on time, no runway settlement, and no airport shutdown. It proves once again that if you give the contractor an opportunity to be creative, the owner can achieve magnificent results.

Waste Treatment and Bottom Ash Project – AES Petersburg Generating Station

This is a $225 million Engineering, Construction and Procurement Project (EPC) and is the largest contract ever performed by Bowen Engineering. We are working under a 50/50 joint venture agreement with Burns and McDonnell out of Kansas City, Missouri. Bowen is responsible for constructability review, commodity procurement, and construction management of direct hire labor and subcontractor coordination. Burns and McDonnell is responsible for the engineering, engineering assistance during construction, management of startup/commissioning and major equipment procurement. This is also the biggest joint venture in Bowen Engineering history.

We had been doing a fair amount of construction for Indianapolis Power and Light, a subsidiary of American Electric Service Co,

(AES) at their facilities in Indiana prior to this project. The Petersburg Waste Water Treatment and Bottom Ash projects came on the radar for future projects. IPL/AES determined that the best delivery method would be an EPC approach. Bowen would not be on the bidders list due to EPC contract methodology

The Bowen rallying cry is, "We never give up." Our marketing leadership of Jeff Purdue and Michael Soller travelled to Kansas City, Missouri to meet with Tom Miller of Burns and McDonnell, who is a Purdue graduate. We had project experience with Burns and McDonnell on more traditional lump sum bid projects. The projects with Burns and McDonnell were very successful and in the process, we developed a good working relationship.

Our two companies agreed to make a run for the project as a joint venture. With Bowen's craft experience at both project sites, Bowen's and Burns and McDonnell's vast wastewater treatment experience, and Burns and McDonnell's strong financial resources, our JV team was able to get on the list of invited bidders. Our competition was a well-known regional contractor and design engineer. We were successful and won the contract. We formed a joint venture, entitled Indiana Water Partners (IWP), and went to work.

Using SQP (Lean principles), we built a $225 million project in sixteen months. We broke ground in the summer of 2016 and the plant was put in service in the summer of 2017. At our peak, we had 450 workers on the job, plus subs. We installed one of the first large-scale remote submerged flight conveyors in the country.

This is probably the most challenging project ever attempted by Bowen Engineering, in terms of size, complexity, and accelerated schedule. We were successful because our marketing guys refused to accept defeat, we had a great joint venture partner, and our employees performed above and beyond expectations. We put our best and brightest on the project, led by Matt Gentry, project manager, and Roger Havill, general superintendent.

The job is important, certainly because of its size, but mostly because it has moved us into the major leagues. Burns and McDonnell is a major player in the power industry. By partnering with them, we have raised our stature. Most large capital improvement projects at power facilities are done by the EPC delivery method which lends itself to a joint venture approach. We have now completed a large scale successful joint venture, and that should add to our reputation. Hopefully, this project will be a door opener to larger joint venture power projects.

We have had a wonderful run of successful jobs and have built a great reputation for quality work, professionalism, and teamwork. John Kupke with HNTB said it best: "It can only get better."

Lessons Learned

- You must grow. You have to be aggressive and take some chances. Status quo will not win the day.
- Never give up. This is true on the golf course, it is true in business, and it is true in construction.
- The owner, designer, and the contractor make a great team. When they work together, everyone wins.

15

REGIONAL OFFICES

"Show me an organization in which the employees take ownership, and I will show you a company that beats its competitors."
– Captain D. Michael Abrashoff, *It's Your Ship*

As a company, you have to ask yourself, are you going to grow or are you going to maintain the status quo? I don't think a company can survive if its goal is to maintain the status quo, if for no other reason than the fact that you have to provide increased opportunities and responsibilities for your management personnel. Most young managers expect to be promoted, their areas of responsibility be expanded, and their personal income increased as they grow in the company. A company cannot provide that unless it is in growth mode. If a company does business as usual, there will be little opportunity to grow people.

At Bowen Engineering, we specialize in the water and energy construction industries. I personally expect that we will be a $1 billion company someday. That is 3.5 times the volume we completed in 2016. There is no way we can grow by 3.5 times, working out of Indianapolis, unless we diversify. We have diversified some. Our performance contracting is managed out of Indianapolis and it has been successful. We will continue to search for other growth opportunities. But that may not provide enough opportunity and advancement for our developed leaders.

We believe that travel will be an essential part of our future playbook. We have two options. Option one is that we build distant projects by traveling from our home office. With this approach, we manage the project by sending out management teams who will live on site during construction and return to the mother ship when the project is finished. We just completed a $50 million power plant project in Kansas City, Missouri. We sent an entire management team there, including project superintendent, project manager, several project engineers, area superintendents, site safety, and site quality. The job went very well and now all of those staff are back home, working on other projects.

This approach works well for our seasoned union superintendents who have been brought up in this kind of construction environment. But it is complicated for our young project managers who haven't been brought up that way, many of whom have young children at home. The only project managers that have left our company in recent years did so because of travel constraints. They did not want to travel.

Option number two is to set up independent regional offices at remote sites around the country. We have made six attempts at setting up regional offices. We currently have an office in Evansville, Indiana, which has been a magnificent success. We are expanding our business there, we have leaders who are well involved in the community, we are profitable, and there is a general excitement about being part of the Evansville office.

We have three other offices that have met medium success; in Crown Point, Indiana, Columbus, Ohio (second try) and in the Washington DC area. These offices are bringing in work and they are profitable. Everyone is active in finding new work and growing the offices, but it is difficult. Our long-term goal is to expand those areas and develop a local presence.

We have had two total failures, in Columbus, Ohio (first try), and Houston, Texas. Both offices were brought down by the non-union labor force. In Ohio, we had to resort to hiring workers from a temporary labor supply company. In the case of Ohio, the mother ship was never totally engaged in supporting the office. Both offices were eventually closed.

What have we learned? We now have a much more developed

strategy for regional offices, including clear key performance indicators (KPI's) defining what success looks like and specifics on what is required from the mother ship to ensure success. This is a work in process and is experiencing continuous change. We have identified several key components to developing solid regional offices.

Our best and brightest talent can live where they want to. Regional offices provide significant career opportunities for advancement. If we can build the work close to the house, we bid it and build it, if it fits our competencies. If not, we will travel for the right fit.

Bowen Engineering's Evansville office

Regional Manager

The regional manager must be a visionary, trusted leader, someone who embraces and models our core values, and someone whom others will follow. He has to be one of the company's best and brightest and well-schooled in the Bowen Engineering culture. He must demonstrate mastery of: 1) leadership skills, 2) Bowen SQP (Lean construction execution), 3) marketing/sales, and 4) what it takes to achieve zero injuries. The manager must want to lead the regional office. He has to care about people. And he has to be global. It is more than just a construction project. He has to get involved in the community and be the face of Bowen Engineering locally.

The regional manager must help the sales (business development) effort. He must be skilled at "hunting and killing" great projects. He must want to grow the business. His most important job is to get good work and grow his people.

The regional manager must be held accountable for performance. The measure of his effectiveness should be an agreed-upon level of performance in safety, quality, hit rate, costs, profitability, growth, and development of talent.

Regional Staff

The regional manager has to have a talented support team that he can depend on and who will follow him. The nucleus of that team often comes from the mother ship. It has to include a superintendent, a project engineer, and a foreman. The regional manager cannot go down alone. He has to know that he can get leadership and support from senior management and support from the home office staff that he can rely on when a tough situation arises, because tough situations will arise. That support can only come from someone who knows the Bowen Engineering way. Having a regional office storefront gives the staff a sense of security and belonging.

Entre

You need a ticket to the dance. That ticket is provided by a great client. You need a great client who has the potential of providing additional work. We set up our Columbus, Ohio office to service American Electric Power (AEP). who was executing a large construction program in the 2000s. Ten years later, AEP had a major cutback in its capital spending and our office had to adjust its strategy. The work we are doing for them now is in southern Indiana and is being managed by our Evansville office because of close proximity.

We also established an office in the Washington DC area, to service American Water Works Service Co. with their major upgrades to the water systems at Ft. Meade and Ft. Belvoir.

This project served as a great anchor project, which is vital for a new regional office. In addition, we had contracts with NRG in Houston, but the Louisiana project did not go well and the Houston projects were cancelled.

Craft Labor

Craft labor is critical. It is fair to say that the craft labor is what brought us down on our first regional office attempts in Ohio and Houston. Bowen Engineering was founded as a union shop. So, when we travel to a remote site, if the area is mostly union, it works beautifully. We have a ready supply of qualified workers available on a moment's notice. We are a strong union company and have excellent relationships with the union leadership.

When we travel to a non-union area, it is more complicated, especially given that our roots are with the union shop. We learned a lot about dealing with the non-union crafts in Houston. The challenges in the non-union arena are: 1) finding qualified craftsmen, 2) keeping them on the payroll, and 3) providing the necessary training to improve their work skills. The problems are: 1) there is a shortage of qualified craftsmen, 2) the workers we hire are often pirated away by other contractors who will provide more hours and higher pay, and 3) the non-union market depends on the individual contractor to provide craft training. Talented craft and field leaders are reluctant to join a new or unknown regional contractor.

When in a non-union environment, it is important to have management personnel who have non-union experience; someone who can help develop a non-union workforce. We now employ a full-time recruiter for non-union workers. This is someone who understands the workforce and our craft needs. In a non-union environment, a contractor must pay well to hire good workers, but it takes more than that to keep them. At Bowen Engineering, we try to sell the idea of family and making the craftsman part of the team. It's working. We are starting to build a cadre of non-union craftsmen who are traveling to some of our remote non-union jobs.

Market Research

It is important to conduct market research to determine if there is enough good quality work to support a new office. It is critical to have an established anchor client or project, but these may not be enough to support an office. If there is not enough good work, the office will struggle to find work. If that happens, the team may bid and win projects too cheaply and that are outside of their expertise.

Sales and Marketing

The new office must have a sales and marketing plan. We have to bring in good work. That requires a sales and marketing team. The sales role can be accomplished using a full-time salesperson or an outside sales consultant. For a small office, an outside consultant might be able to provide the necessary sales effort. The mother ship should provide its best sales and marketing resources to help develop the regional office sales and marketing plan. The regional manager must also be involved and be a part of the sales and marketing team. Everyone is a salesman. That is especially true in a regional office.

The regional office marketing plan should include:

- A formal sales funnel with established financial targets for sales leads, suspects, and prospect projects.
- An established annual bid volume based on an assumed bid hit rate.
- A list of targeted A-B-C clients, engineers, vendors, and subcontractors to call on to identify good projects.

The best marketing a company can do is to delight its clients. This is especially true for a new regional office that does not have the luxury of being known.

Support from the Mother Ship

The mother ship must decide if the regional office makes sense. This decision must depend on market potential, labor force, and clients. It cannot be an emotional decision. It must be based on the facts as we know them and must answer the question, "Do we have an anchor client?"

We have to set realistic expectations for the regional office. If we start out too small, it is not worth the investment. If we start too large and too fast, we lose control, make bad decisions, and lose employees.

The mother ship must be "all-in" and must provide as-needed support in terms of marketing, estimating, heavy equipment, human resources, safety, and financial management. At Bowen Engineering, all checks and financial accounting for the regional office are handled in central accounting. The regional manager must report to a senior manager in the main office who is engaged and will support and hold the regional office accountable.

Business Plan

There should be a business plan that includes expected revenue, gross margin, overhead, net profit, return on investment, safety performance, sales and marketing plan, and customer satisfaction. The plan should be revisited and updated annually and the regional manager must be held accountable for it.

Local or Regional Presence

We must develop a local or regional presence/reputation. Local owners want to know that their contractors will be there to help solve problems. We need to run our projects effectively, but we also need to expand our horizons. We need to think globally. We need to be involved in several activities:

- **Network in the industry and community.** Participate in the local chamber of commerce and AGC chapters by finding a subcontractor or vendor who can host us.
- **Building relationships with vendors and subcontractors in the area.** We must make personal visits to their offices and ask them to help us network.
- **Developing an identity in the community and industry.** At the regional office, we are not part of the mother ship. We are a standalone independent business. Letterhead should show the regional address, not the home office.

Our Evansville office is a good example of how to engage in the community. Jeff Purdue is active in area service organizations. He is also teaching engineering at a local high school. The office has been successful because we have created an identity. We have created a lot of excitement and people in Evansville know our management team. Building a positive reputation is not easy; it is a big challenge.

Esprit de Corps

Everyone on the team has to love being part of the new office, and they have to show it. They have to love being out on their own, so to speak. We have to develop a sense of family. Our Evansville office has an annual summer party and Christmas party for employees and their families. Esprit de corps is also part of having a global perspective.

Charter

If the plan is to move forward and start a new regional office, draw up a charter or an agreement. The charter is for all to see and agree to. It simply sets out all of the above strategies. If a new project engineer arrives from the main office, he signs the charter. He now knows what the plan is and how he will fit in. Not very complicated, but at least we all have the same vision.

Bowen Engineering works in an ever-expanding geographic area. We try to service our clients, our company, and our employees. Regional offices do this. But they are not a guarantee. When we select a project to pursue and staff, we ask the following questions:

- Where is the job located?
- What is the availability of project leadership?
- What is the skill level needed for the project?
- Are there client relationships that can be enhanced?
- What is the workforce availability?

We will probably start a new standalone office in the future. Our regional manager will be a seasoned Bowen Engineering professional and experienced in managing a non-union work force. We will have a customer who will potentially award us a fair amount of work. Our team members will be leaders in the community and the local construction industry. This expansion is important for our future. We cannot miss.

Lessons Learned

- If a company is going to travel, it must get craft labor under control.
- The regional office has to break away from the mother ship.
- A regional office has to have the best and brightest people in the company to run it.

- A regional office needs an anchor project and/or an anchor client that can be a source for work.
- The management team must broaden its horizons and think globally.
- The regional management team must have realistic goals and must be held accountable.

Acknowledgement:

I received considerable help on this chapter from Bowen senior managers, Jeff Purdue, John Dettman, Ed Storrs, Pat Stanford, and Jameson Pearson. They collaborated and helped me organize and develop the content. They have been actively involved in our regional offices.

16

EMPLOYEE STOCK OWNERSHIP

*"Make employees partners...reward them with stock
ownership, a stake in the business."*
– Bill Lyles, III., President, Lyles Diversified, Inc.

I was a stockholder in California, when I worked for the W.M. Lyles Company. I paid $7,500 for my stock and sold it back to the company when I quit, for $15,000. The Lyles family loaned me the funds to buy the stock. I was really proud to be a stock holder and paid the loan off as quickly as I could. Mrs. Lyles told me that I paid the stock loan off quicker than any previous employee. I thought it was a great way to do business. And I thought this is how great companies operate.

It was a natural evolution that I would sell stock to my employees. I approached the idea early in our history. Interestingly, my outside CPA and my banker both tried to talk me out of it. They said minority shareholders would put undue pressure on me and drive me crazy.

At Lyles, the shares of stock were priced at book value. When I sold my stock back to the company, the share price was book value the day of the sale. Bowen Engineering started selling stock in 1970, and to appease the bank and our outside CPA, we priced the stock shares at a multiple of earnings. We used the average earnings per share over the last three years and multiplied that number by six. If the average earnings per share for the last three years was $2.00, we sold the stock for $12.00 per share. If the stock was bought back, we used the same formula. The price per share using the multiple of earnings approach was about twice as expensive as using the book value approach. In about 1972, we changed the formula to book value.

I thought that the Lyles system was outstanding. I thought this is the way a business should be run. We were no different than IBM or General Motors. We were a business. This was not my own personal investment fund.

You can argue that our stock price was a bargain because our price-earnings ratio today is about four, while the price-earnings ratio of the stock market is about sixteen. And you would be right. Our stock is underpriced. That was the opinion of the bank and our CPA. But our employee/stockholders are more than just passive investors. They are also investing their blood, sweat, and tears. How do you price that?

You can argue that a construction business is different from other businesses. A privately held construction business is a closely held company because you can't buy shares in the open market. At Bowen Engineering, you have to work there to own stock.

The earnings potential in the general economy is market driven and economy driven. The earnings potential of Bowen Engineering is driven by the hard work and dedication of its employees. I am familiar with a large general contractor who is on the New York Stock Exchange. In 2010, they made record profits and their stock price went down 25 percent, thanks to the vagaries of the stock market. At Bowen, if we make record profits, our stock price will go up 25 percent. The only vagaries at Bowen Engineering are how hard and smart we want to work.

Our employees purchase stock at book value. Dividends are paid each quarter. Since we are a sub S corporation, they must pay taxes on corporate income as individuals. The dividends are designed to cover estimated tax payments and provide some profit distribution. If they leave the company, the stock is purchased back by the company at book value. The payment is made through a five-year promissory note earning interest at commercial rates.

Being a sub S corporation adds some government regulations to the process. We can have a maximum of one hundred shareholders.

As of this writing, we have seventy-five shareholders. If we go over one hundred, we lose our sub S status. We then would be a C corporation and would have to pay corporation taxes. And the individual stockholders would pay taxes on the dividends, or double taxation. At some point in time, we will bump up against the one hundred stockholder ceiling. CEO Doug Bowen will have to figure out how to deal with that.

The long-term objective is that our employees will own 50 percent of the corporate stock. The balance of the stock will be owned by the Bowen family. The family stock has voting rights and the non-family stock is non-voting. Our stock ownership structure is not unlike that of the Bechtel Corporation, the largest privately-held construction company in the world. They are family and employee owned.

When it comes to employee stock ownership, I think Peter Kiewit, Peter Kiewit and Sons, says it best:

> *"One of the reasons our results are better than our competitors is that all of our stock is owned by employees – people who are actively engaged in our business. Each one is a part owner of our company and is, in a sense, working for himself. Certainly this should provide a definite incentive to our employees and a corresponding benefit to the company."*

Who gets to own stock at Bowen Engineering? If you are a super star and/or an up-and-comer, you will be offered the opportunity to buy stock. Generally, a new employee is offered stock no sooner than three years after being hired. All of our senior managers and most of our project managers are stockholders. Many of our project engineers and superintendents are stockholders.

I know of no other company that sells stock to superintendents unless it is through an employee stock option plan (ESOP). Most companies will not sell stock to union members. Many of our superintendents are union members and we are proud to include them in the roll of stockholders. They contribute significantly and they need to share in the rewards.

Buying company stock can be a sizable financial challenge for our young project engineers and project managers. They all have families and other major purchases such as cars and homes. To ease the financial burden, Bowen Engineering offers corporate loans to the employees to assist with their initial stock purchases. We charge commercial interest rates and expect the employee to pay the loan off in a reasonable time period.

As time goes by and the employees achieve a higher level of responsibility and success, we offer additional shares to their original stock ownership. We are careful to monitor their stock loan balance so that we don't create an unfavorable burden on their financial condition.

Doug Bowen, Bowen Engineering's CEO, believes that we would not have survived fifty years if we had not sold stock to our employees. We have done many things well, but I believe employee stock ownership is the Holy Grail. Our senior managers and project managers get calls from head hunters regularly. One senior manager told me of a call from one of our competitors in Indiana. He told the caller that he was a stockholder at Bowen Engineering. The caller said that was not an option at their company.

Let's visit the minority shareholder dilemma. Over the years, we have sold stock to over one hundred employees. Probably two dozen have left the company or retired. We have had no problems with any disgruntled stockholders, and one or two were rather complicated and could have been difficult. The benefits of having sold stock to our employees far outweighs any damage or inconvenience that might have been created by one disgruntled stockholder.

Our employees invest their careers, their families, and their financial security in Bowen Engineering and they give maximum effort. It is appropriate that they share in the ownership and rewards generated. They know that we care and are willing to share our company with them. We have very little turnover from our key management staff.

It begs the question, how has employee stock ownership impacted my own personal wealth? I can own 100 percent of a smaller company, or no company at all. Or my family can own 50 percent of a much larger company. Which is greater? I think it is a no brainer. When you sell stock to your employees, everybody wins.

We believe that the stock purchase program has solidified our company and provided long-term employees. Our strategy is that they will spend their careers here. When they retire, we hope they look back and feel like they were part of a family, that they made a difference, and can enjoy the fruits of their efforts. Some of our employees have retired as millionaires.

Lessons Learned

- We are employee owned.
- Construction company stock should be priced at book value.
- Set up the company in sub S status.

17
ZERO INJURIES

"Culture drives operational excellence, which in turn drives organizational success."
– David B. Wells, World-Class Safety Program

Contractors are faced with an age-old dilemma. They are focusing on productivity and making a profit. Many feel that spending time on safety takes away from productivity and the bottom line. In reality, a good safety program promotes productivity and effective work processes.

A serious workplace injury or death changes lives forever. The human loss and suffering are immeasurable. Every person who leaves for work in the morning should expect to return home in good health. Can you imagine the knock on the door to tell you that your loved one will never be returning home? Or the phone call to tell you that he's in the hospital and will never walk again?

Our job as leaders, professionals, and quality-minded contractors is to ensure that husbands return to their wives and parents return to their children. That is the most important reason to create a safe and healthy work environment. But that isn't the only reason; here are a few others:

- **Reducing injuries reduces cost to your business.** The obvious costs are lost time, medical costs, increased worker's compensation premiums, and possible OSHA fines. But equally damaging are the effects on crew morale and productivity and on the project leadership who has to deal with damage control and the complexities of the accident. A single injury can have far-reaching and debilitating effects on your business.

- **Safe workers are loyal workers.** We conduct daily safety huddles for every employee and crew. We seek out our workers' opinion on safety matters. They know that their opinion counts and that as a company, we are listening. I hear repeatedly from our employees that we are the safest contractor that they have ever worked for. They love working at Bowen Engineering. They know that we care. This engenders trust, commitment, and pride in their jobs. And they work harder.
- **Safety improves quality.** A safe workplace tends to be more efficient, free of debris and cord tangles. By working in a clean environment, workers can reduce distractions and truly focus on quality. Better, safer projects create customer loyalty.

Safety starts at the job site. Every worker on every crew participates in a daily huddle before work begins on every Bowen project. It is led by the foreman and the agenda is safety, quality, and productivity. A job safety analysis (Fig. 1) is prepared each day and is signed by each crew member. Potential safety hazards are identified, and actions are agreed upon to eliminate or manage same. Each crew member is admonished to stop work if they see an unsafe situation on the job site. Our safety metrics have improved since we started daily huddles.

We have truly developed a safety culture. We have won two Silver Eagles, awarded by the Indianapolis Construction Round Table. The Silver Eagle is awarded to the company that has the best safety program/record for the calendar year. Our employees tell us that they have not worked for any other contractor that takes safety as seriously as Bowen Engineering.

From a purely business perspective, our private owners also want a safe jobsite. If we are going to work in the private market, we have to be a safe contractor. Today's owners are increasingly focused on quality. They are also concerned about their image in the eyes of their workers and the community. So, they are driving a safe jobsite.

Zero Injuries

Form 005-5.2-01

JOB SAFETY ANALYSIS (JSA)

SUPERVISOR/FOREMAN: _____ WEATHER CONDITIONS: _____

DATE: _____ TIME: _____ AM / PM PROJECT: _____

TASK GENERAL DESCRIPTION: _____

Stored Energy Types: ☐Pressure Tests ☐Overhead Loads ☐Concrete Pours ☐Electrical ☐Excavations ☐Other:

PERMITS
☐ Confined space
☐ Hot Work
☐ Clearance_____
☐ Excavation_____
☐ Grating removal
☐ Other_____

PERSONAL PROTECTIVE EQUIP
☐ Normal PPE
  -Hard Hat
  -Safety Glasses
  -Safety Work Boots
☐ Fire Retardant Clothing/Arc Flash Protection
☐ Gloves_____
☐ Additional Foot Prot:_____
☐ Face Shield
☐ Goggles
☐ Respirator/Dust Mask
☐ Hearing Protection
☐ Fall Protection_____
☐ Seat Belts
☐ Sharp Objects
☐ Welding Shield
☐ Welding Sleeves
☐ Mono-goggles
☐ Mechanical Vibration
☐ Other_____

TOOLS
☐ Daily Inspection
☐ Proper Tool(s) for the Job
☐ Proper Cutting Tool for the Job
☐ Grinder Gaurds/Handles in Place
☐ Grinder/Grinder Wheel Speed Compatable
☐ Air Hoses Secured
☐ Cords, Handles, Guards
☐ Pipe Plug (ex. Inflatable, Expandable)
☐ Other_____

EMERGENCY INFORMATION
☐ Fire Hose
☐ Fire Extinguishers
☐ Safety Shower/Eye Wash Station
☐ Evacuation Route/Reporting Area
☐ MSDS Review
☐ Emergency Phone Location
☐ Safety Cans, Labels
☐ Other_____

FALL PROTECTION
☐ Safety Harness_____
☐ Proper Anchorage Point(s)
☐ Lifeline
☐ Personnel Platform (or Man-basket)
☐ Daily Inspections
☐ Handrail (top – mid - toe)
☐ Proper Barricade/Signage
☐ Lanyard/Retractable_____
☐ Other_____

EXCAVATIONS
☐ Properly Barricaded with Signage
☐ Shoring Required
☐ Proper Access/Egress
☐ Inspected by Competent Person
☐ Other_____

WELDING
☐ Condition of Welding Leads/Machines
☐ Combustibles
☐ Welding Screens
☐ Fire Blanket
☐ Fire Extinguisher Available & Inspected
☐ Proper Clothing/ Sleeves, Jackets
☐ Welding Hood
☐ Welding Gloves
☐ Fire Watch
☐ Other_____

ELECTRICAL
☐ GFCI Test
☐ Grounding
☐ Extension Cord Inspections
☐ Electrical Tool Inspected
☐ Adequate Lighting
☐ Lockout / Tagout
☐ Other_____

HOUSEKEEPING
☐ Access/Egress/Walkways Clear
☐ Organize Extension Cords
☐ Designated Storage Area(s)
☐ Proper Stacking of Materials
☐ Other_____

PLANTS AND ANIMALS
☐ Poison Ivy/Oak
☐ Snakes, Animals, Insects, Birds
☐ Other_____

SCAFOLDING / LADDER /LIFTS
☐ Inspected & Tagged by Competent Person
☐ Special Provisions:_____
☐ Tied Off
☐ Access Ladder/Inspected/Secured
☐ Aerial Lift Pre-Use Inspection
☐ Other_____

GENERAL
☐ Flammable
☐ Asbestos
☐ Lead
☐ Arsenic
☐ Heat stress
☐ Hole Covers
☐ Slip/Trip Hazards
☐ Dust, Fume/Smoke Protection
☐ Rebar Caps
☐ Proper Barricade/Signage (ex. Pressure Test)

HEAVY EQUIPMENT / HOISTING
☐ Critical Lift
☐ Crawler/Hydrolic Crane(s)
☐ Inspected
☐ Proper Maintenance
☐ Operator/Oiler in Place
☐ Outriggers Extended
☐ Signaling Method_____
☐ Manual Lifting Equip._____
☐ Proper Rigging Practice
☐ Personnel Platform Prelift Form
☐ Overhead Hazards_____
☐ Voltage_____
☐ Safe Working Distance_____Ft.
☐ Safe Travel Distance_____Ft.
☐ Proper Barricade/Signage (ex. Swing Radius)
☐ Tag Line(s)
☐ Controls to be Used
  ☐ Backup Alarms
  ☐ Use Air Horn When Swinging
  ☐ Spotter
  ☐ Other_____

STEEL ERECTION
☐ Stability Provision for Temporary Support
☐ Jacking (as needed)

Safe Work Dist. (Ft)	
Voltage	Distance
0-50 kv	10'
50-200 kv	15'
200-350 kv	20'
350-500 kv	25'
500-750 kv	35'
750-1,000 kv	45'

Safe Travel Dist. (Ft)	
Voltage	Min. Dist.
0 - 0.75 kv	4'
0.75 - 50 kv	6'
50 - 345 kv	10'
345 - 750 kv	16'
750 - 1,000 kv	20'

By signing this JSA, I acknowledge and declare that I did not have an injury, did not witness an injury and did not witness any incident and/or accident during the course of today's work with Bowen or its subcontractors. Any injury or accident that I witnessed or became aware of was immediately reported to Bowen's superintendent or safety representative.

	PRINT NAME	SIGNATURE IN	SIGNATURE OUT	AT-RISK
1.				
2.				
3.				
4.				
5.				
6.				
7.				
8.				
9.				
10.				
11.				
12.				
13.				
14.				
15.				

Revised January 2014

Fig. 1 Job safety analysis (JSA) - page 1

It Takes More Than Concrete

JOB SAFETY ANALYSIS (JSA)

LIST SPECIFIC TASK STEPS	LIST POTENTIAL HAZARDS	LIST ACTIONS TO ELIMINATE OR MANAGE HAZARDS

PRIOR TO STARTING WORK - Evaluate the line of fire and "what if". (Ex. What if the channel locks slip...Could they hit me? A co-worker? Could it cause me to lose my balance? Make me fall?) Have this discussion to determine what can happen if... and plan/proceed accordingly.

Have you checked and discussed with other crews in or around your work area to see if they have hazards that could affect you? Y or N or NA

When the plan changes S.T.O.P.P.

Foreman Signature: (AFTER Completed Review)_____Date / Time:_____

*MANAGEMENT "FELT PRESENCE"AUDIT SUPERVISOR: _____ Date / Time: _____

End of Shift Inspection:

Housekeeping: _____ Holes Covered: _____ Signage: _____ Work Area Secured: _____

Lock-Out/Tag-Out: _____ Straps Stored Properly:_____ Safety Equip. Stored:_____ Heavy Equip. Secured:_____

Supervisor / Foreman_____ Date / Time:_____

Job safety analysis (JSA) - page 2

They are holding contractors accountable. Unsafe contractors will not be hired.

For years, the industry standard for measuring a company's safety performance was the Experience Modification Rate or EMR. The EMR is an adjustment multiplier of the company's worker compensation rates and a measure of a company's safety performance.

EMR calculations look at total payroll and the worker's compensation loss record over the last three years. It then compares that loss record to the industry average. If a company has a loss record greater than the industry average, it will have an EMR greater than 1.0. That EMR is then multiplied against standard worker's comp rates and the company's worker's comp insurance costs go up. Conversely, if the loss record is below industry average, the multiplier is less than 1.0. The corresponding insurance costs go down. This can have a major impact on a company's cost of doing business. A company with a lower EMR has a cost advantage over the company with a higher EMR.

If a company has a major accident or fatality, the impact on the company's worker's comp insurance lasts for three years. This further exacerbates the cost implications of the accident. Not only does a company have the loss and anxiety of the accident, but the cost impact lasts three years.

Our EMR has consistently been between 0.54 and 0.71 in the last ten years (Fig. 2). This means that we have a distinct cost advantage over contractors who are not as safe. But if we can achieve zero injuries, our EMR will be even better. Our objective is to lower our EMR. The best-of-class contractors will achieve at or below 0.50 EMR.

Owners look at EMR, but it is not the primary measure of a company's safety performance. Today, the industry measures safety performance by the Total Recordable Incident Rate (TRIR). A recordable incident is any accident on the jobsite that requires medical attention beyond first aid and/or causes a loss of work time. A TRIR of 1.0 means that you had one recordable incident for every one hundred workers in a one-year period. Pretty daunting.

Today's private owners require their contractors to have a TRIR of less than 2.0. If you want to be a preferred contractor, your TRIR must be below 1.0.

Our TRIR was 2.47 in 2006, but we did primarily public works projects and the owners were not too concerned about safety or the TRIR. Today, we do almost 90 percent private owner construction. You can see in Fig. 3 that our TRIR has improved over the years and was 0.93 last year. If we had a 2.47 TRIR today, we would be out of business. Conclusion? Disregard safety at your peril.

BOWEN ENGINEERING CORPORATION

TEN YEAR SAFETY METRICS

YEAR	2006	2007	2008	2009	2010	2011	2012	2013	2014	2015	AVERAGE
HOURS WORKED	1,130,325	1,653,116	2,111,960	1,944,606	1,371,688	1,633,278	1,439,902	1,444,271	1,458,550	1,449,214	1,563,691
EMR	0.64	0.67	0.71	0.62	0.57	0.55	0.54	0.56	0.63	0.68	0.62
TRIR	2.65	1.57	1.33	1.85	1.31	1.35	0.69	0.69	0.82	0.97	

Fig. 2 Safety figures TRIR & EMR

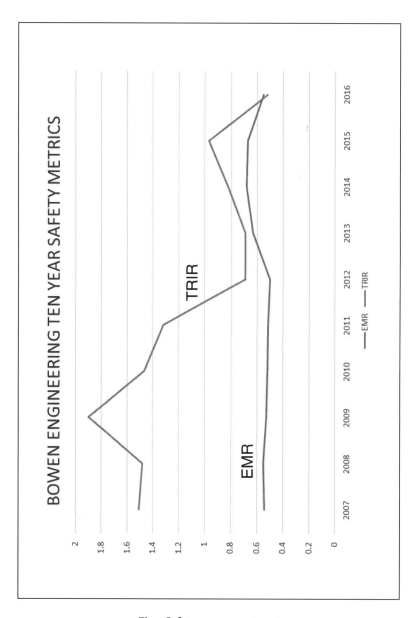

Fig. 3 Safety curves 2006-2016

At Bowen Engineering, we have developed a strategy for running a safe jobsite and a safe company. Our senior management team has come up with safety rules to live by:

1. **Safety is a culture** – Safety is not a department. It is not a program. It defines the way we do business. Everyone from the CEO to laborer is committed to safety. It is a condition of employment. We have terminated seasoned veterans for poor safety practices.
2. **Zero injuries** – The title of our safety program is Zero Injuries. Our goal is to have zero accidents on our jobsites. We have not been able to do that in any year yet. We have had many jobs without any recordables.
3. **Safety director reports to the CEO** – Our safety director reports directly to our CEO, Doug Bowen. If you want to run a safe company, it starts at the top.
4. **All meetings begin with safety** – Whether it is a board of directors' meeting or a beginning of shift meeting, the first item of the agenda is safety. Everyone knows it and everyone lives it. No exceptions. All of our field crews start the morning with a safety huddle.
5. **Safety has no budget** – We will spare no expense to provide a safe jobsite. Our safety director knows that when someone on the jobsite needs a special tool, he gets it, no questions asked.
6. **Safety orientation** – All new hires go through an extensive training orientation. At our Kansas City project, we have a special trailer dedicated to zero injuries. In the trailer are twenty-five safety stations. It takes a new hire four hours to go through the entire safety orientation.
7. **Safety training** – All project managers, project engineers, and superintendents go through safety training each year. This is part of our regular project manager and superintendent meetings.

Travelers is our insurance carrier. They have developed the Travelers Safety View Perception Survey. It is a simple, straightforward online survey, to help contractors evaluate their safety management systems. The Survey includes questions about "best safety management practices"—the ideal practices found in outstanding safety management systems. The results help identify specific improvement opportunities. The Survey measures employee perceptions of safety management practices in these key areas:

- Accident investigation
- Employee involvement
- Safety training
- Hazard identification and correction
- Post-injury management
- Supervisor involvement
- Safety communications
- Visible management commitment

The Survey takes twenty minutes. Travelers provides quantitative data about the effectiveness of your safety management system. It is a great way to engage your employees and improve safety management. You can get more information at:

Travelers Indemnity Company
One Tower Square
Hartford, CT 06183

Safety is about awareness and attitude. It isn't about following procedures. It is staying alert to possible hazards, taking the extra time, and even stopping the work process to ask questions. We have developed a four-step process that our workers are expected to live by:

1. **Focus** – Focus on the task and concentrate on the job. If you become distracted, you are in danger of making a mistake and an accident can happen.
2. **Strength** – It is not muscle power. It is the strength to do the right thing, when you are under pressure to take shortcuts. A good safety attitude means you have the strength to stick with procedures, even when no one is looking.
3. **Time** – A good safety attitude means taking the time to do things correctly. Is saving a few minutes worth a lifelong injury? If you add up the costs of injuries, it is cheaper to do the job the right way the first time.

4. **Responsibility** – If you care about yourself, your family, and your co-workers, you will take responsibility even when the task "isn't my job." Think of yourself as part of a team.

So many construction companies think that safety is an extra expense. We have found that our safest jobsites are our most productive. We believe that a safe jobsite promotes better productivity.

Zero Injuries has become a movement at Bowen Engineering. All of our employees are expected to commit to that movement. We even hold commitment ceremonies on each jobsite to celebrate it. A major part of our success is that we run a safe jobsite. Our employees know that we as a company care about them. They don't care how much you know until they know how much you care. It must be part of every activity. It defines the way we do business.

Lessons Learned

- To be a truly safe company, you must develop a safety culture.
- The CEO must be on board.
- Safety has no budget.
- All construction activities start with a safety moment.
- Safety training and orientation programs must be part of the management strategy.

18
AGC OF AMERICA

"You find out that in every community, the contractors are all alike. It is a family affair, they are all good people."
– Richard Pepper, executive, Pepper Construction

When I started my company in 1967, one of my goals was to join the Associated General Contractors of America (AGC) (see chapter three). My dad had been a member of the AGC highway chapter in Indiana, but I don't remember him being active. Lyles and Kaweah were not members of AGC. They were members of the Engineering and Grading Contractors Association (EGCA). I don't know how I was introduced to AGC, but I knew that was where the big boys played, and I wanted to be part of it.

Soon after I signed the Bowen Engineering corporate papers, I applied to join AGC of Indiana. Guess what? I was rejected. They said I hadn't built any projects, therefore I couldn't join as a contractor. No problem. I built a couple of jobs and reapplied. I was accepted and joined AGC in 1970.

Why does someone join a contractors' association called AGC of America? Here are some of my basic reasons:

- **To have a voice in government.** The congress and legislature regularly pass legislation that impacts our industry, and they are not contractors. Through AGC, we are able to educate and express our views and concerns before legislation is passed.

175

- **Labor union representation.** Bowen Engineering is a union contractor in Indiana. AGC leads multi-employer bargaining with the local construction trade unions.
- **Professional development and education.** AGC has developed the Supervisory Training Program (STP) and several programs on Lean Construction. Those are just a few of the many training programs for the contractor.
- **Rubbing shoulders with the leaders of the industry.** Every time I attend an AGC meeting, I learn something new that impacts my company. Many contractors establish joint venture arrangements by their contacts through AGC.
- **Maybe the most important reason is stated in the AGC logo.** Skill, integrity, and responsibility; these are the bywords of AGC. There is a quality and value proposition that goes with being part of AGC.

Owners have always held retention on contractors' monthly payments, which is usually 10 percent. Legislation was passed, thanks to the AGC leadership, that required retention dollars on government jobs be placed in escrow and that the interest generated be for the contractor's account. That happened thirty years ago. The impact this had on Bowen Engineering is immeasurable.

I was a young and opinionated contractor. I was not included in the union bargaining. One day, I was asked to serve on the carpenters' bargaining committee. Tippy Wilhelm, of Wilhelm Construction, was committee chairman. The carpenters were asking for a $2.00/hour raise over three years. The contractors wanted to offer $1.00. I suggested in the committee meeting that we should only offer fifty cents and that was too much. Three years later, when bargaining came up again, I was not invited to be on the committee. Many years later, I became chairman of the carpenters' bargaining committee. I showed them. I offered $1.00/hour.

Micro tunneling rig in bore pit - Evansville, Indiana

In 1980, we began in-house training for our foremen and superintendents. We used the AGC STP program as our resource material. The AGC even provided instructor training. I attended the training and was asked to be a member of the national STP committee. Through STP, we discovered preplanning. The first material we used was written by Mike Casten. If it hadn't been for AGC, we would never have discovered preplanning, would never have met Casten and Dave Pedersen, and would not be using Lean Construction today. How important is that?

I can still remember an AGC of Indiana convention trip to Mexico City. My wife and I had dinner with Paul Schiele, Bill Shook, Jerry Kerr, and Bob Jesse and their wives. Here I was, a nobody, having dinner with the icons of the Indiana construction industry. That is something I will never forget.

The STP committee led me to get more involved in national AGC education. Paul Diederich, education committee chairman, started the Project Manager Course (PMC) in Dallas in 1990. I was on the faculty and taught preplanning. The course is still going strong and I have taught the class since the beginning. I have taught almost one hundred classes. So, when Dean Jameson called in 2010 and asked me to teach a class in construction engineering and management at Purdue University, I was ready. Thanks to AGC, 2018 will be my eighth year teaching at Purdue.

I have played a lot of leadership roles in AGC. My most important was president of the AGC Education and Research Foundation. I stepped down in 2017. Under my watch, we implemented faculty residencies and developed industry case studies for the college classroom. This has been one of my proudest honors.

The story just gets better. Bowen Engineering has won seven Build America Awards:

- 1999 – Wastewater Treatment Plant Expansion - Village of Peotone, Illinois
- 2000 – Sewer Rehabilitation Project – Evansville, Indiana
- 2003 – Phase II Water Systems Improvement – Michigan City, Indiana
- 2005 – Wastewater Treatment Plant Expansion – City of Lafayette, Indiana
- 2007 – Cinergy Gibson Station Flue Gas Development
- 2008 – Citizens Thermal Energy Indianapolis Airport Utility Connector
- 2016 – Citizens Thermal Energy Group Southport Waste Treatment Plant Expansion

These awards were the top utility projects in the nation for their given years. They are the Oscars of the construction industry.

Wastewater Treatment Plant - West Lafayette, Indiana

The heart of AGC is its motto: skill, integrity, and responsibility. This value proposition permeates every AGC activity. Everywhere you go, AGC is promoting those great American values. I am so proud of AGC. It has had a huge effect on me personally and on Bowen Engineering.

Lessons Learned

- Be a player. Don't sit on the bench.
- Giving back is good business.

19

OUTSIDE BOARD OF DIRECTORS

*"If a company does not have an outside board of directors,
the president ends up buying his own bad ideas."*
– Leon Danco, The Center for Family Business,
Cleveland, Ohio

Do you want to be a mom and pop operation, bidding and building projects and adding up the costs at the end of the year, or do you want to be a professionally run business and a player in the market and the industry? Bowen Engineering is a full-fledged professional corporate business. In many ways, we are no different from General Motors or IBM. Having an outside board of directors is consistent with that model.

W.M. Lyles and Kaweah Construction in California both had outside boards. Bill Brown, president of Kaweah, had me meet with some of his board members. One board member was the president of the local utility in Visalia, California. He wasn't an expert in construction, but I think he brought knowledge of finance, the market place, and the community. Brown was very proud of his board members.

In the early years, our board was made up of my dad, my mom, and my wife. We had irregular board meetings that were usually attended by my dad, Jack Crane (our outside CPA), and one or two senior managers. We had an agenda and addressed issues. But let's face it; I was running for my life and didn't have a lot of time for board meetings.

I attended a seminar on family businesses presented by Leon Danco with The Center for Family Business in 1982. Danco proposed that every company should have an outside board of directors. This forces the president to sell his ideas to an independent body. Otherwise, bad ideas may go unchallenged. Corporations are designed to have boards of directors. This is just good business. The absence of a board creates a carelessness in running the business. I never thought that our initial board was the most professional way to do business. So, I was an eager student when I heard Danco.

We established our first outside board in 1985. Our board members were Dick Gabrielse, a contractor I had worked with in the Associated General Contractors of America (AGC), and Lee Lamb, a senior manager at Guepel DeMars Construction, a local Indianapolis contractor. Lamb had also worked at Wilhelm Construction, another local contractor and we were pretty good friends. Both board members had significant construction experience. Was it a board made in heaven? No. But it forced me to organize my thoughts and make a presentation to an outside independent group every quarter. We were beginning to look like a professional organization.

Gabrielse shared with me his experience working for a mechanical contractor in Michigan. He said the contractors' bonus pool was set at 25 percent of their annual net income. I liked the idea, and we implemented a 25 percent bonus pool at Bowen Engineering. That bonus pool is still in effect today and has served us very well. We would not have set up the 25 percent bonus pool if we had not had an outside board of directors.

In 1988, we added Larry Hannah, at the suggestion of our attorney, Tom Withrow. Hannah had been a senior manager with American Fletcher National Bank in Indianapolis. He remained on our board for twenty-five years. He had also served as president of MacAllister Machinery, the local Caterpillar dealer. Then in 1990, we added Jerry Kerr, a retired senior manager with Huber, Hunt and Nichols Construction, a national firm located in Indianapolis. He served on our board until 2007.

Our early boards were made up of contractors and bankers. They provided us with good counsel and we began to develop a board mentality. All of our employees knew, and I think respected, our outside board members.

Kerr connected us with a project manager from Huber, Hunt and Nichols. We hired the project manager and then bid and won the twenty-three story Conrad Hotel in Indianapolis. We could not have built the Conrad Hotel if we had not had an outside board of directors.

Each of Bowen Engineering's board members is paid a stipend. They are expected to attend four board meetings and five audit/ investment committee meetings per year. They are also given the opportunity to purchase company stock. They are all stock holders.

I learned a lot about running a board from Richard Pepper, chairman of Pepper Construction in Chicago. He suggested that I sell stock to our board members. It was a good idea. He also told me about the time when he had made an important company decision without consulting the board. The board walked into his office and resigned in mass. They said that if he could make that kind of decision without consulting the board, he didn't need a board.

I stepped down as president in 2000 and the board elected Jed Holt, COO of Bowen Engineering, as our new president. I became chairman. From that point on, we had six board members; three individuals inside the company, chairman, president, CFO, and three outside members.

The board elected Doug Bowen president in 2006 and CEO in 2010. Over time, he has brought in his own board members; Dave Pedersen, Tag Birge, and Robert Welch. Pedersen is a construction management consultant we had used for many years, Birge is a lawyer and real estate developer in Indianapolis, and Welch is an investment banker from a long line of investment bankers in Indianapolis. We had leaders from various segments of industry and they each brought in an expertise that enabled our company to grow and prosper.

The chairman and president must make the board strategy work. It takes some effort on their part to communicate with and engage the board members. Nothing is automatic. It is important to communicate with them and keep them in the loop. It is important to seek out their opinions, especially when making an important company decision. They must be part of the family.

On one occasion, three of our middle managers had quit. The outside board took our CEO aside to challenge company management. They were concerned. Even though I was on the board as chairman, they didn't tell me about their concerns. I was dismayed, but decided that maybe I needed to spend a little more time with my outside board members. I now do just that. I try to meet with them between board meetings, one-on-one.

All of our board meetings are attended by senior management. The board is able to discuss the ongoing activities of the business and challenge management as needed. The senior managers are actively engaged and the interplay is very effective.

We have an audit/investment committee that weighs in on our cash management. The committee's most important function is to manage dividend payments. The group meets when tax estimates are due.

Many companies have boards, but they are often made up of company employees and owners. I have one friend who owns an engineering company and has an outside board, but they don't meet. In general, our competitors do not have outside boards.

We have had an outside board since 1985 and it has been an important part of our success. If anything, we have built a professional corporation and we are good business people. Having an outside board is good business.

Lessons Learned

- It pays to have an outside board of directors.
- Board members should be compensated and given the opportunity to purchase company stock.
- Communication is not automatic. The chairman and president must engage the board members.
- The chairman should stay in touch with the outside board members outside of board meetings.

20

FAMILY BUSINESS

"The beauty of a family business is that it provides stability.
The employees want to know that the company is stable."
– Bill Dudley, CEO retired, Bechtel Corp.

Bowen Engineering is a family business. We believe that this is the best way to insure the company's future. We don't do this to line the pockets of our heirs. The primary consideration is Bowen Engineering. We believe that there is no better candidate to take over the business than the natural offspring, if he/she is talented, dedicated, and skilled in the art of running a business.

Albert Douglas Bowen III was elected by the board to be our third president in 2006. He was then promoted to chief executive officer in 2010. Under his leadership, we celebrated our best year ever in 2016. The senior management and the employees have supported him wholeheartedly. As a result, we have truly developed a leadership culture. The employees will more quickly support the family heir than they will an outsider. They are looking for stability.

According to the Family Firm Institute (http://www.ffi.org):

- 30 percent of family businesses survive into the second generation
- 12 percent survive into the third generation
- 3 percent survive into the fourth generation and beyond

I use the Bechtel Model. Bechtel is the world's largest privately-owned construction company. They are now in their fifth generation and Brendan Bechtel is CEO. I asked Bill Dudley, retired Bechtel CEO, if the company was in any danger because the new CEO was so young. He said, "Brendan is smart and talented and he has a strong team of experienced leaders around him."

For my part, I feel truly blessed to have my son step in and run the business. However, at times it has been difficult. I founded the company and it was my own personal fiefdom. I thought I still had some value and good ideas, learned from running the company for forty years. Doug was new to the role of CEO and he took my suggestions as criticism. He had enough stress from running the business. The last thing he needed was more stress from me.

I have learned to step aside and let Doug run the business. Martin Jischke, president emeritus at Purdue University, told me, "When you retire, you must know your self-worth and keep your mouth shut." I have learned to do that. We conduct one-on-ones and Doug consults with me and includes me in Bowen activities. But it is his company and he is running it. We have developed a pretty good relationship. That is very important to the employees. I couldn't be prouder.

Doug has done a very good job. He has developed a thorough job cost monitoring system, expanded and developed leadership skills in our upper and middle management, and has had to negotiate some very complicated claims and settlements. But his most important contribution is that he supports and maintains the core values that were established by Tom Greve, Jed Holt, and Bob Bowen thirty-five years ago. That is the beauty of the family business. When you bring in an outsider to be president, he will want to make his mark and the first thing he will do is change the core values. Doug supports and promotes our core values, perhaps, better than the old timers did.

Bowen Engineering Core Values

- Service to the customer, above all else
- Never walk away from a problem
- Excellent and ethical business practices
- Continuous improvement

- Enthusiastic teamwork and celebration
- Shared opportunity and ownership
- Highest commitment to a safe workplace
- Genuine concern for others

One family member will be the boss. It will be his business and he will control the stock. We have four kids. We did not divide the pie into four equal pieces. You cannot run a company by committee; someone has to be in charge. Business experts will tell you, do not divide the pie evenly between the kids.

We have a succession plan. All of the grandkids have been told that they must: 1) get a college degree, 2) work somewhere else when they graduate from college, for at least three years, and 3) have a responsible leadership position. Then they can join the family business.

The family owns 50 percent of the company. The employees own the other 50 percent. The family stock is voting stock, and non-family stock is non-voting. No one can own stock unless they work in the company. That goes for family and non-family.

Tousley-Bixler was the primo builder in the mid-eighties in Indianapolis. The company was employee-owned and was being run by the third generation of employee leadership. My bond underwriter, Dick Peterson, said the company would not survive. He said, "You cannot run a company by committee." My opinion was that they were run like a major corporation and would be very successful. Dick was right. They did not survive. That lesson has stuck with me over the years.

In Asia, most businesses are family businesses. In America, most businesses are non-family. You can make the argument that Asians are focused on the long view and what is sustainable. Americans, conversely, are focused on the short view; what can you do for me today? If the Asian family has a daughter, she is expected to marry someone who will work in the family business. Most of the famous Asian businesses that we recognize are family run.

Most American businesses are for sale. The owners want to cash in for big bucks. The strategy is flawed. They are trading in a business in which they are the expert for a cash/investment program in which they are not the expert. Now they have to manage money, which is not easy. They are also giving up an exciting lifestyle, in which they were actively involved, for a passive lifestyle. I have a lot of friends who have sold their businesses and are not very happy. I have a friend who sold his business when he was in his late forties. We had dinner one night and he said, "Bowen, tomorrow morning when I get up, I will have nothing to do." I thought, "Wow, that wouldn't fit my lifestyle." Fifteen years later, he and I were playing golf. He said, "Bowen, retirement is not what it is cracked up to be."

One of my heroes is Thomas Watson, Jr. at IBM. He took over from his old man and certainly added to an already excellent business success and reputation. I have friends who were IBM executives. They will tell you that it was a shame that Watson Jr. didn't have an heir who could step into his shoes and run the company.

There are many reasons why a family business survives:

Stability – The employees have staked their lives, careers, family, and security on the company. They want and deserve to know that the company has a solid strategic plan and a stable future. They want to know that the company is in good hands. The family business provides that.

Long-term perspective – The family heir will take the long view, in terms of strategic planning and decision making. He/she knows that his leadership has to stand the test of time. Conversely, the non-family president will be watching the short run, because he knows that is how he will be measured.

Continuation of core values – When Randy Tobias took over Eli Lilly Company as chairman and CEO, he did not change any of the company's core values. He enhanced them. Tobias will go down as one of Lilly's most successful and remembered CEOs. That is happening at Bowen Engineering.

Employee loyalty – I just believe that the employees will follow the family heir better than the non-family leader. For one thing, there are complicated politics with the non-family leader. The politics with the family heir are much less complicated. The employees know the plan and will make it work. Look at all of the wonderful ideas presented in this book. They come from our wonderful, dedicated employees. It is working.

Trust – Maybe this is our family's by-word, or should be. Trust is knowing that there is a plan, the leadership is competent, and that the leadership cares about its employees. When you have trust, you will build a successful business.

Better cash management – The family has the biggest stake, so they should manage the cash well. Doug Bowen includes me on many cash management decisions. Am I the world's greatest cash manager? No! But I have been around for fifty years and have learned a thing or two.

The family business is beautiful. I am truly blessed to have my son run the company. I know of many companies that have failed because the founder and the heir couldn't get along. Doug and I work hard at developing a working relationship. It is his company and he has to run it. I know my place. I know my self-worth and I keep my mouth shut, unless asked. This is very important to the employees. The employees must perceive that Doug and I are working well together. Absent that perception, they will lose confidence in the company and the company leadership. It is vital to our survival.

Doug Bowen will have to learn this same lesson when his heir steps into the limelight.

Lessons Learned

- You cannot run a business by committee.
- Employees are looking for stability.
- Employees are generally loyal to the family heir.
- The family heir will take the long view. That is important.

Doug Bowen on wind turbine - Brookston, Indiana - 2008

21
FIFTY YEARS

"Great leaders have no more than five driving strategies
that they live by in their businesses because if everything is
important, then nothing is important."
– Randy Tobias, retired chairman and CEO,
Eli Lilly and Company

The construction industry has to be the greatest industry in the world. No other industry provides the challenges, the excitement, and the rewards that construction does. Every project is exciting, challenging, and different. No project is the same. I attended a speech by Overton Currie, with Smith, Currie and Hancock, Atlanta, which is probably the leading construction law firm in the world. Currie just loved working with contractors. He said, "They put their life, their estate, their family, and values on the line every day when they sign that next contract." I personally thank God that I ended up in construction.

Construction is tough and it is unique. It is not like making widgets. Contractors must defend against weather, labor unions, government regulations, bank covenants, owner non-payment, and market downturns, just for starters. It is no wonder that all of our competition from 1967 is out of business. But it is great if you can handle it, and if you're tough.

How do you survive for fifty years? What are the difference makers? Below are the five strategies that have had the biggest effect on my success and on our company's survival:

1. **Employee Stock Ownership** – The biggest differentiator is that we have sold stock to our employees. None of our original competitors did. Our top employees get calls from headhunters regularly. The first question my employee will ask is, "Can I buy stock in the new company?" The answer is no. Our stockholders get a dividend check every quarter. I don't know of another company who sells stock as deeply into the management staff as we do, unless they are an employee stock option plan (ESOP). We even sell stock to our best superintendents. Why other contractors haven't adopted our model is astonishing.

2. **Positive Attitude** – The second differentiator is esprit de corps. I can honestly say that I have become more positive as I have gotten older. As a result, I am happier, a better leader, and more successful. There is only one way to become more positive; by making the conscious decision to change your behavior. All of our employees are expected to be members of the Compliment Club. This has certainly helped build our culture. You will be a better leader the more positive you are.

3. **Planning/Lean Construction** – We were introduced to planning in the AGC Supervisory Training Program in 1980. Today, we teach planning for the AGC Project Manager Course. We are the acknowledged leaders in the planning process. Today, our planning has embraced Lean Construction. We are experiencing unbelievable results in improved productivity and performance, thanks to Lean. Our owners, partners, and subcontractors recognize our expertise in planning. It has become a culture.

4. **Marketing is Everything** – If we had not developed our marketing/sales program that we have today, Bowen Engineering would probably not be in existence, this book would never have been written, and you would never have heard of Bob Bowen. It has certainly had a major impact on the success of our company. Performance contracting, which is going so well, is the result of excellent marketing. Our involvement in the power market is also the result of excellent marketing. And don't forget, everyone is a salesman. Marketing has become an important part of Bowen Engineering's culture.

5. **Leadership** – Everyone is looking for leadership. Today, we have a hundred leaders at Bowen Engineering, people who are making a difference. I didn't dream up all of the wonderful ideas presented in this book. They came from our creative, dedicated, young leaders. I often wonder what role I played in the success of Bowen Engineering. I did not create these good ideas. If anything, I gave our employees the freedom to be creative and excel. I wanted every employee to have an opportunity to do an outstanding job.

Bowen Headquarters - Indianapolis, Indiana

In the year 2000, we had been in business for thirty years. Even though we had stockholders, we were in reality, an entrepreneurship. It was my company and I ran the business. My fingerprint was on just about everything. I had studied a case at Harvard where the founder had run the business until he died. He had no succession plan, no management transition, and left a vacuum in the company management. I didn't want that to happen at Bowen Engineering, and I also thought it was time that we began to operate like a true corporation.

To that end, we promoted Jed Holt, who was COO at the time, to president. That was probably a fortuitous move. I think we made a statement. We sent a message to the entire company that anyone can rise to the top. It only takes creativity, hard work, and leadership.

When I was a young president of the company, probably thirty years ago, my daughter Kris gave me a book on goal/priority setting. I don't even know why I read it, but I did. I set my five life priorities. I have listed them here, *in order of importance:*

1. Bowen Engineering Corporation
2. Terry L. Bowen (wife)
3. Kids (and grandkids)
4. Good health
5. Giving back

Bowen American crane located at headquarters front lawn.

Commitment to Work and Family

If you are going to be a champion, you must be totally focused. Vince Lombardi said it best: "God, country, and the Green Bay Packers." My family knows that Bowen Engineering is my number one priority. It has been said that life balance is important. I agree. But my family must understand that my career will impact their lives, and it has. When I was a young president of the company, I worked constantly, but I spent every spare minute with my kids. I coached my son's football, baseball, and basketball teams. He said he appreciated it but that I wasn't a very good coach. Hey, we were league champs in football, runners-up in baseball, and we upset the top basketball team in overtime one year! I remember riding bikes to swim practice with my daughter at 6:00 am. I cut my grass one time in my adult life. That was the first time and the last time. From then on, I hired the kid next door, for ten dollars. I spent that time with my kids instead. I was not a great parent, but I worked at it. Tom Shelby, president of Kiewit Energy Group, was a guest speaker at the class I teach at Purdue University. He said he doesn't cut the grass. He has better things to do.

Commitment to Good Health

My son once told my wife that I spend a lot of time staying young. I think that to stay young, you must do three things: have a positive attitude, keep your brain active (by doing things like writing a book), and keep your body active. What did I learn in physics at Purdue? A body in motion tends to stay in motion. John Wooden, probably the greatest basketball coach of all time and Purdue legend, walked five miles every day. He lived to ninety-nine, and was cognizant on his death bed. Stay engaged and keep moving.

Bob and Terry Bowen at the finish line of the
Plainfield, Indiana Walk for Water 5k.

Commitment to Giving Back

Martin Jischke, president of Purdue University, said that
giving back is an essential part of leadership. We have all been
blessed. I think we are obligated to share our good fortune with
as many people as possible. I want to give young people the same
opportunities that I had, in terms of education, work opportunities,
good values, and genuine concern for others.

My wife, Terry, and I started our family foundation in 1994.
We have awarded 800 hundred scholarships totaling $3 million
to African American college students in Central Indiana. She is
chairman of the foundation and has done a wonderful job. Each of
the four kids has one seat on the board. When Terry and I are gone,
they will run the foundation. Terry and I are the lead contributors
for the Robert L. and Terry L. Bowen High Performance Civil
Engineering Laboratory at Purdue University.

Robert L. and Terry L. Bowen Laboratory for Large-Scale Civil Engineering
Research - Purdue University

Our young managers are engaged in community. Jeff Purdue,
Bowen Engineering's vice president of business development,
served on the board of Junior Achievement and started high school
engineering clubs in Evansville. Project managers Matt Gentry and
Mark Cvetkovich both organize annual golf tournaments in their
communities to benefit local charities. Alan Dale, project manager,

serves on the Construction Management Advisory Board at Ball State University. He also serves as guest speaker in their classes.

Bowen Engineering does a lot work for Citizens Thermal Energy in Indianapolis. Mark Jacobs, COO of Citizens, approached Doug Bowen to enlist financial support for the United Way of Indiana. Doug said we could do that, but he also asked if our two firms could do a joint community service project for United Way. That was four years ago. To date, Citizens Energy and Bowen Engineering have rebuilt and upgraded the playgrounds for four community centers in the Indianapolis area. The work is completed by the management and staff of both companies. How is that for giving back?

The YMCA and United Way are important. But more importantly, these community involvement activities tell me about the character and values of these young people. It tells me that they care about others. That personal involvement impacts their leadership skills and the success of Bowen Engineering.

Parting Thoughts

As I finish this book, my parting thought would be that we have to take ownership of our lives. Bill Smith, former vice president of construction for Eli Lilly, said, "I don't want any victims." If you have a problem, let's talk about solutions, or a response, or an action plan. No "woe is me."

I had a pretty unspectacular life in high school and during my first two years at Purdue. I developed into a fairly good student in my last two years, making A's and B's and raising my GPA to a 3.0. Low and behold, I was invited to rush Chi Epsilon, the civil engineering honorary fraternity. I was dumbfounded. I couldn't believe that I was going to be a member of an honorary fraternity.

Not so fast! I was rejected by the fraternity. I was not asked to join. I think my lifestyle from my first two years at Purdue was not consistent with their sensibilities. I was crushed. I had just gone from the high point in my life to the lowest point in my life, in one second. I will never forget the disappointment.

I did not sit around feeling sorry for myself. (I did a little.) I went to see the faculty advisor, Frank Stubbs. He also headed up construction in the school of civil engineering. I didn't get into Chi Epsilon, but I did make a friend and mentor in Stubbs. I think he felt sorry for me. When W. M. Lyles came to Purdue to interview potential graduates, he asked Professor Stubbs to recommend three students to interview for a job. Guess what? I was one of the three and I got the job.

If those Chi Epsilon boys hadn't held me accountable, and I hadn't taken ownership of my life and gone to see Stubbs, there would be no Bowen Engineering. My step-son Brian Stater says it best: "Don't ever give up." He is talking about golf, but it is also true about life. Interestingly, in my later years, I was inducted into Chi Epsilon as an honorary member.

I have had many challenges and successes in life. I have certainly had disappointments, but I think they molded me and made me a better man. I wouldn't want to go back and change a thing. They say success in life is not in how hard you fall, but how you get up. We built a great company. It has been due to the efforts of some wonderful employees. They are truly my heroes. I am so honored to have been a part of this team and company.

The story stops here, but doesn't end here. My message to our young managers and leaders is to carry on the esprit de corps. That is the thing that makes us most unique. Our family plans to continue to lead the company to the future. The good news is that it can only get better.

REFERENCES AND RESOURCES

"Decoding of Inconsistent Communications", Albert Mehrabian and Morton Wiener, *Journal of Personality and Social Psychology*, May 1967.

Fails Management Institute (FMI Corporation) Pricing and Bidding Strategy Seminar: http://www.fminet.com.

Family Firm Institute (succession planning resources): https://www.ffi.org.

"Inference of Attitudes from Nonverbal Communication in Two Channels", Albert Mehrabian and Susan R. Ferris, *Journal of Consulting Psychology*, June 1967.

International Leadership Associates (Kouzes and Posner leadership training): 2 Sheila Court, Hamilton, Ohio 45013, 513-755-7112.

It's Your Ship: Management Techniques from the Best Damn Ship in the Navy, Captain D. Michael Abrashoff, Grand Central Publishing, New York, 2006.

Kiewit: An Uncommon Company: Celebrating the First 125 Years, Jeffrey L. Rodengen, Write Stuff Enterprises, Inc., Fort Lauderdale, FL, 2006.

Lean Construction Institute (training resources): 1400 North 14th St., 12th floor, Arlington, Virginia, 703-387-3050.

Lean Restructuring Participant's Manual, First Edition, AGC of America, Arlington, Virginia, 2012.

"Marketing is Everything", Regis McKenna, *Harvard Business Review*, January/February 1991.

Pepper Construction: Beyond Bricks and Mortar, A Proud Seventy-Five Year History and Heritage, Ann B. McGowan, Printing Arts Chicago, Cicero, IN, 2003.

Power vs Force: An Anatomy of Consciousness, David M. Hawkins, MD, PhD, Hay House Inc., New York, NY, 2012.

"Social Intelligence and the Biology of Leadership", Daniel Goleman and Richard Boyatzis, *Harvard Business Review*, September 2008.

The Associated General Contractors of America (AGC): https://www.agc.org.

The Leadership Challenge: How to Make Extraordinary Things Happen in Organizations, James M. Kouzes and Barry Z. Posner, Jossey-Bass, San Francisco, CA, 2007.

The Toyota Way: Fourteen Management Principles from the World's Greatest Manufacturer, Jeffrey Liker, McGraw-Hill Education, New York, NY, 2004.